POPE FRANCIS
AND OUR CALL TO
JOY

DIANE M. HOUDEK

D0062058

Franciscan
MEDIA
Cincinnati, Ohio

to
FR. HOWARD HAASE,
whose compassion and inspired preaching first spoke to me
of the joy of the Gospel and continues to do so,
and to
POPE FRANCIS,
who renewed that joy and is proclaiming it throughout the universal Church.

Excerpts from *Evangelii Gaudium* (The Joy of the Gospel), © LIBRERIA EDITRICE VATICANA, are used with permission. Scripture passages have been taken from *New Revised Standard Version Bible,* copyright ©1989 by the Division of Christian Education of the National Council of the Churches of Christ in the U.S.A., and used by permission. All rights reserved.

Cover and book design by Mark Sullivan
Cover image © Reuters/Tiziana Fabi/Pool

LIBRARY OF CONGRESS CATALOGING-IN-PUBLICATION DATA
Houdek, Diane M.
Pope Francis and our call to joy / Diane M. Houdek.
pages cm
ISBN 978-1-61636-849-4 (alk. paper)
1. Francis, Pope, 1936- 2. Christian life—Catholic authors. 3. Church and the world. I. Title.
BX1378.7.H68 2014
248.4'82—dc23
2014016002

ISBN 978-1-61636-849-4

Published by Franciscan Media
28 W. Liberty St.
Cincinnati, OH 45202
www.FranciscanMedia.org

Printed in the United States of America.
Printed on acid-free paper.
14 15 16 17 18 5 4 3 2 1

CONTENTS

PREFACE, *v*

A Year of Pope Francis

INTRODUCTION, *ix*

St. Francis, Pope Francis, and Our Call to Joy

CHAPTER ONE, *1*

"We Have Found the Messiah" | *Discovering Jesus in the Gospels*

CHAPTER TWO, *11*

"Mud on Our Shoes" | *The Church Meets the Real World*

CHAPTER THREE, *23*

"All Are Welcome" | *Gathering with Others as a Community of Faith*

CHAPTER FOUR, *29*

"Don't Let the Devil Steal Your Joy" | *Overcoming Obstacles and Resistance*

CHAPTER FIVE, *42*

"Let Us Begin Again" | *Returning to the Word of God*

CHAPTER SIX, *49*

"Blessed Are the Poor" | *The Special Place of the Poor and Vulnerable*

CHAPTER SEVEN, *60*

"Stewards of Creation" | *Peace and the Common Good*

CHAPTER EIGHT, *67*

"The Kingdom Is Here" | *A Renewed Impulse to Share Our Faith*

A YEAR OF POPE FRANCIS

The year 2013 marked several firsts for the Catholic Church and in particular for the institution of the papacy. On February 28, Pope Benedict XVI announced his plan to resign his office as pope. While not a first, it was the first in a long time, certainly in the modern history of the papacy. He also cleared the way for the cardinals to gather sooner rather than later to elect his successor. It was likely the Church would have a new universal leader by Easter. Catholic news organizations were overflowing with stories of the front runners and who might be elected and why and what this would mean for the future of the Church. Many of the network news organizations got into the swing of the papal election to fill the gap left by the end of the U.S. presidential election campaign.

I was tired of politics, tired of campaigns, tired of stories of who's in and who's out. I have always had a low tolerance for in-fighting and factions, especially in Church organizations and institutions. The polarization in the Church between liberals and conservatives has increased exponentially with the rise of the Internet. Blogs and social media and an increasing number of online publications, all with comments and discussions and their attendant trolls, has meant that what might have been a few people talking about how the Church— or parish—is being run is now a ceaseless din of a thousand voices.

I had my own opinions about how the papal election might turn out. I had been pleasantly surprised by Pope Benedict's tenure. He was far more pastoral as pope than he had been as the long-time head of the Congregation for the Doctrine of the Faith. I watched as the U.S. media rooted for local favorites on the short list. I listened to those who thought a return to power by the Italians was inevitable after a Polish and a Bavarian pope. I dismissed those who thought that the prophecies of St. Malachy, the Irish Nostradamus, dictated that the next pope would be the last and Rome would be destroyed—although Cardinal Turkson, with the prophetic first name Peter, was one of the leading candidates. I watched with amusement as college basketball's March Madness brackets and the European and Irish betting professionals seemed natural ways to handicap the "race."

What struck me in all of this commotion was that I had come to believe that it really was just another form of power and politics and all the corporate baggage that comes to accompany any human institution. I knew enough about the history of the papacy to know that the "princes of the Church" had often been as corrupt and power-hungry as the kings and princes of the secular world—and often from the same families. Some of the current jockeying for position was coming from the way the press—both secular and religious—were interpreting events. They were spinning it in a context they understood. But just as the conclave was beginning, I was struck by the realization that I honestly wasn't sure I believed that the Holy Spirit played any part in this selection of the head of the universal Church. I had fallen prey to one of the dangers of working for the Church. I had let my inside awareness become nothing but cynicism. And it disturbed me because I also knew that the future direction of the Church would have a real and practical impact on my own work as a

Catholic writer and editor. I suddenly realized that a lot was riding on this conclave, for me as well as for the Church.

At about this point, a friend on Facebook posted a link to a website that was randomly assigning people a cardinal to pray for during the conclave. Of course I clicked on it, partly thinking it was a worthwhile effort and partly wondering if God's sense of humor would ensure that I would be assigned to pray for someone I had previously criticized. I got my response, and it was a cardinal from South America, Jorge Mario Bergoglio from Buenos Aires, Argentina. I was intrigued and Google led me to Wikipedia, where I discovered that he was a humble man who lived in a simple apartment, did his own cooking, and rode the bus to work. At work the next day I told several coworkers about this cardinal who seemed so refreshingly simple and committed to justice for the poor. I continued to look for information about him and discovered that he had actually been second in the voting in 2005. So he wasn't as much of a dark horse as I might have expected.

As news of impending white smoke made its way through our various live streams, we drifted toward the Franciscan Media conference room to wait for the announcement. I was astounded when it turned out to be "my" cardinal. The announcement that he was taking the name Francis resonated with those of us gathered together that day. I had just finished a book of daily reflections based on the writings of St. Francis. And my college education had been entrusted to the Jesuits. Many threads of my life as a Catholic were coming together in this historic moment. I texted my spiritual director that he would be relieved to hear that I was going to be able to stay Catholic! More than a few cynical journalists and publishing professionals were filled with new hope in those first moments after the election of the new pope. It was more than a sense of relief that the worst hadn't happened. It was a genuine sense of excitement, possibility, new opportunities. We were filled with joy! And that joy has not abated in the year since then.

St. Francis, Pope Francis, and Our Call to Joy

Following the example of his namesake, St. Francis of Assisi, Pope Francis has made joy one of the hallmarks of his papacy. It's a joy in the simple things in life and a focus on sharing God's love with everyone he meets. It's a way of looking at the world that sees hope and possibility, that emphasizes real connections over the distance that can accompany formality.

Joy is deeper than mere happiness. It is less influenced by external circumstances. Events and people and material things can make us happy. But if we bring an inner disposition of joy to our lives, we will be surprised by the way we can change the people around us. When we describe someone as "joyful," we often mean that they bring a special light into life. We know that we aren't always going to be happy. Sadness, even tragedy, is going to cross our paths more than once. But if we strive to be joyful on a daily basis, we seem to develop reserves upon which we can draw.

Our faith is tested at difficult times. Sometimes we drift away when things are going well. Tragedy, doubt, and stress can bring us back. Other times we have a surface belief, but when things get tough, we need to dig deeper for a new kind of faith. Sometimes the greatest joy comes in realizing that we have come through a time of trial and we recognize that it's God's grace that has enabled us to persevere.

One of the greatest obstacles to understanding, living, and sharing the joy of the Gospel is that too often the Christian message has been cheapened by facile clichés until "God loves you" has the same depth of meaning in our lives as a smiley face and "Have a nice day." If our actions don't show that love to others, our words will fail to reach them. If we don't have an awareness of what that love means through times when others have listened to us and loved us through our pain, then we will find it difficult to believe that God loves us.

Perfect Joy

One of the best ways to look at the importance of joy is through the story of St. Francis and his quest for perfect joy. In a dialogue with his friend Brother Leo, he talks about coming home to the friary cold, tired, and hungry, and having the door slammed in his face. He knocks again and asks to be admitted but the refusal escalates to outright violence. He tells Brother Leo that if he can endure such humiliating treatment without reacting in kind, that would be perfect joy. This story is often misunderstood as seeking out the most miserable circumstances as a path to sainthood. But what the saint is showing is the ability to maintain an inner equanimity and joy no matter what is happening around him. He is modeling his behavior on Jesus's experience of hanging on the cross and forgiving those who had placed him there, giving them the benefit of the doubt that they "know not what they do." Perfect joy is the ability to return peace and love to those who cross us. That is indeed the path to sainthood, and few of us manage to walk it perfectly.

A quick search through the writings of St. Francis of Assisi will reveal hundreds of references to joy and a joyful life. This doesn't surprise us, because we usually think of St. Francis as an especially joyful saint, surrounded by all God's creatures, making music, rejoicing in all kinds of circumstances. One of my favorite stories of St. Francis comes from his first biographer, Thomas of Celano. He tells us:

> St. Francis maintained that the safest remedy against the thousand snares and wiles of the enemy is spiritual joy. For he would say: "Then the devil rejoices most when he can snatch away spiritual joy from a servant of God. He carries dust so that he can throw it into even the tiniest chinks of conscience and soil the candor of mind and purity of life. But when spiritual joy fills hearts," he said, "the serpent throws off his deadly poison in vain. The devils cannot harm the servant of Christ when they see he is filled with holy joy. When, however, the soul is wretched, desolate, and filled with sorrow, it is easily overwhelmed by its sorrow or else it turns to vain enjoyments." (193)

It's not surprising that Pope Francis's first apostolic exhortation is entitled The Joy of the Gospel (*Evangelii Gaudium*). The document echoes and elaborates on many of the thoughts and reflections we've been hearing from Pope Francis throughout his first year as pope. More than that, however, the warmth and welcome in his actions and the enthusiasm with which he has embraced his new role as Bishop of Rome and pastor of the universal Church has brought a smile to so many faces and a feeling of hope to a weary Church and a cynical world.

Evangelization is far from a new idea in the Church. But he hopes that this exhortation will mark the beginning of a new chapter, "pointing out new paths for the Church's journey in years to come." (1). Building on the work of his predecessors, Pope Francis brings the gift of a pastor who is clearly in touch with his people. This message is coming from one who walks with the people, whether in the slums of Buenos Aires or the streets of Rome. He has taken to heart the message of opening to the Spirit that was first expressed by the Second Vatican Council and is showing us how to take that message to the world.

Vatican II's Constitution on the Church in the Modern World"carries the Latin title *Gaudium et Spes* (Joy and Hope). It was the attempt by the Council to engage the world not in an adversarial relationship in which the Church was right and everyone else was wrong, but with a recognition that God's truth was something that could be found in the most unexpected places.

One of the most divisive areas in the Church today is the way we as Catholics approach the culture around us. Vatican II and now Pope Francis remind us that we can see the world through a lens of joy and hope. Too many Catholics and other Christians have begun once again to reject all that happens outside the Church walls as sinful and even evil. Pope Francis has shown that we don't need to hide behind barricades in the culture wars. We can offer people a real sense of possibility and life instead of merely condemning those things that lead to death. It's a shift of focus from pessimism to possibility, from fear to hope, from death to life.

Perhaps the most significant thing to keep in mind when we think about the prominence of joy in the lives of St. Francis and Pope Francis and our own call to joy is that its source is a deep and abiding awareness of God's love for each and every one of us. If we trust that God loves us as individuals, as we are, we can't help but be filled with joy. If we know that we ourselves are loved, it becomes much easier to see that God loves those around us as well.

Pope Francis has often spoken of the glum countenance that Christians sometimes reveal to the world, and how much that kind of attitude gets in the way of sharing the joy of the Gospel. But he also recognizes that our lives can at times be dark and difficult. The message of Jesus is that even in those moments, we can experience the joy of the resurrection:

> There are Christians whose lives seem like Lent without Easter. I realize of course that joy is not expressed the same way at all times in life, especially at moments of great difficulty. Joy adapts and changes, but it always endures, even as a flicker of light born of our personal certainty that, when everything is said and done, we are infinitely loved. (6)

I think I especially resonate with this passage, but it was just this kind of revelation of God's love that turned my life around. We all have moments in our faith lives that mark a turning point, a particular conversion. For me it was an Advent reconciliation service in the midst of my second year of graduate school. I had been pushing myself academically for months and meeting both "failure" (OK, it was a B in my Shakespeare class) and frustration and envy of the people around me who seemed to care far less than I did about their classes and yet seemed to get ahead of the game effortlessly. I wanted to be recognized for what I knew, for what I could accomplish. So when my confessor said, "You are loved and lovable simply because God created you," it stopped me in my tracks.

Until that moment, I don't think I knew that I was looking for love. And by placing it in the context of God's love, it was someplace where human failings and imperfections and imperfect expectations couldn't limit it. It might have been the first time that I considered what it would be like to be loved for who I was and not for what I could do. Looking back to that moment after almost thirty years, I can now see that I heard those words differently both because of the grace of the moment and because I was receptive to the message. Part of the reason for that receptivity was that I was desperate. Nothing else was working and I knew it.

Few people can go through the ups and downs of daily life with an unrelenting sense of happiness. We go through a whole range of emotions, moved by our own doubts and feelings of inadequacy, our anger at the actions of others, our fear of what the future might hold, and at times our despair at our own sinfulness. Pope Francis reminds us that at the heart of the Gospel message is the truth that as many times as we fall, God is there to pick us up again: "How good it feels to come back to him whenever we are lost! Let me say this once more: God never tires of forgiving us; we are the ones who tire of seeking his mercy" (3).

Those who are motivated primarily by fear of God find it difficult to believe that God truly loves them as they are. They always think that they need to be better, do better things, in order to earn the love of a demanding and never-satisfied parent. If we know that we are loved, we want to be better just because we know that we can do more and be more and find new life in that love. Knowing that we are loved doesn't make us complacent. It spurs us to share that love with those around us. It's not something we achieve and cross off our list; it's something we are.

This sense of utter dependence on God is something that is especially difficult for those who are taught from an early age to depend on themselves, their own efforts and talents, and to depend on those who can help them get ahead in the world. Pope Francis recognizes this when he speaks of the special joy he finds among the poor:

> I can say that the most beautiful and natural expressions of joy which I have seen in my life were in poor people who had little to hold on to. I also think of the real joy shown by others who, even amid pressing professional obligations, were able to preserve, in detachment and simplicity, a heart full of faith. (7)

It can be easy to dismiss words of hope and encouragement as clichés, as Hallmark sentiment, as Internet memes. Those of us who constantly erect walls around our vulnerability don't want to be seen as foolishly optimistic or hopeful. We approach happiness and its deeper expression of joy as naïve and simplistic. We think it's fine for children, but we're adults, and we know how easily we can be hurt. It takes someone special to break through those barriers and encourage us to trust the joy. Jesus was able to do that. He told his disciples that unless they became like children—vulnerable and defenseless—they could not enter the kingdom of God. St. Francis spent most of his life delighting with childlike simplicity at the world around him. Pope Francis is showing again and again that he has that gift as well. What can we learn from him about making that gift our own?

> Thanks solely to this encounter—or renewed encounter—with God's love, which blossoms into an enriching friendship, we are liberated from our narrowness and self-absorption.... For if we have received the love which restores meaning to our lives, how can we fail to share that love with others? (8)

No one can strip us of the dignity bestowed upon us by this boundless and unfailing love. With a tenderness which never disappoints, but is always capable of restoring our joy, he makes it possible for us to lift up our heads and to start anew. Let us not flee from the resurrection of Jesus, let us never give up, come what will. May nothing inspire more than his life, which impels us onwards! (3)

Throughout his exhortation, Pope Francis acknowledges that the Church itself has sometimes been an obstacle in sharing the Good News:

The joy of the Gospel is such that it cannot be taken away from us by anyone or anything (cf. Jn 16:22). The evils of our world—and those of the Church—must not be excuses for diminishing our commitment and our fervour. Let us look upon them as challenges which can help us to grow. (84)

I don't always want to hear that the answer is to keep the faith and see it as a challenge to grow. But sometimes it helps just to know that the difficulty is real and that I'm not alone in the temptation to despair and declare defeat. A wise pastor used to remind us, "What you focus on, you give power to." Pope Francis reminds us to keep our focus on the joy, not the pain: "The Lord does not disappoint those who take this risk; whenever we take a step towards Jesus, we come to realize that he is already there, waiting for us with open arms" (3).

What is it about Pope Francis that makes us want to listen to him? What is it about his call to evangelization that makes even the most shy and introverted among us think that maybe this time it might be possible? It might be that by his example he's showing us step by step how to do it. Even the earthiness of his interviews and his writing make it possible for him to reach people who wouldn't normally read an encyclical or apostolic exhortation. Those of us on the inside of ministry and theology like to talk about how significant these documents are. But the average Catholic (and, truth be told, a good many professional Catholics) don't really take the time to put the words into practice.

Pope Francis comes to the papacy out of a solidly pastoral background. His writing doesn't lose touch with that. He knows that the Church and its teachings have to make sense in the real world, not just in academic conferences.

An evangelizing community gets involved by word and deed in people's daily lives; it bridges distances, it is willing to abase itself if necessary, and it embraces human life, touching the suffering flesh of Christ in others. Evangelizers thus take on the "smell of the sheep" and the sheep are willing to hear their voice. (24)

The cross Francis wears as pope is the same one he had as archbishop and cardinal of Buenos Aires. It depicts Christ as the Good Shepherd, carrying the one sheep home accompanied by the rest of the flock. This is a man who understands what it means to seeks out the lost, the confused, the disillusioned, the weary.

Whenever our interior life becomes caught up in its own interests and concerns, there is no longer room for others, no place for the poor. God's voice is no longer heard, the quiet joy of his love is no longer felt, and the desire to do good fades. This is a very real danger for believers too. Many fall prey to it, and end up resentful, angry and listless. That is no way to live a dignified and fulfilled life; it is not God's will for us, nor is it the life in the Spirit which has its source in the heart of the risen Christ. (2)

Francis, like the best spiritual directors, knows when to comfort and when to challenge. When he sent seminarians out to work with the poor, he checked their shoes for dust when they returned. He has a heightened sense of hypocrisy, of pretense, of spiritual complacency. And yet he also has demonstrated incredible patience with those who have fallen from the straight and narrow path. Like Jesus, he can challenge in different ways both those who believe they are perfectly holy and those who are afraid they are beyond redemption.

A Letter from the Pastor to his Flock
From the time of St. Paul, Church leaders have stayed in touch with their communities through letters. Whether resolving problems or encouraging the faithful in good times and bad, these letters tell us something about the leaders and something about their communities. In our own time, we have seen a number of pastoral letters from our bishops as well as more formal documents from the Second Vatican Council. Popes generally issue either encyclicals or apostolic exhortations. In the first year of Pope Francis's papacy we've seen one of each. The encyclical The Light of Faith was issued at the conclusion of the Year of Faith and was a combined effort by Benedict and Francis. The Joy of the Gospel is a response to the 2012 Synod on Evangelization, a gathering of the world's bishops in Rome.

Recent popes beginning with Paul VI in the 1960s have been encouraging the faithful to take up the task of evangelization or spreading the Good News about Jesus with admittedly mixed results. For a variety of reasons, Catholics are uncomfortable with the concept of being a missionary or evangelizing people. They think of missionaries as people who go to foreign countries and preach the Gospel to pagans and savages. Or they think evangelization means going door to door with tracts and proof texts, much as the Jehovah's Witnesses and Mormons do. Then there are the televangelists encouraging their viewers to accept Jesus into their hearts as their personal Lord and Savior—and if they're so moved, to mail a check to the evangelist. There's a deep-seated sense that Catholics don't do any of these things. We go to church on Sunday, we celebrate the sacraments at appointed times in our lives and the lives of our children, we pray alone or with our families, and in the decades since Vatican II, we increasingly read the Bible. We might go to events at our local parishes (especially the Lenten fish fries or weekly Bingo). It can be a stretch to get involved in a Bible study group or a small faith-sharing group. Our Catholic identity might be personal, social, or cultural.

The apostolic exhortation "The Joy of the Gospel" is addressed to "Bishops, Clergy, Consecrated Persons and the Lay Faithful" (that's everybody, folks!). While there are several sections addressed to priests and lay ministers, most of it applies to ordinary Catholics. We want to look at ways in which the pope's encouraging words can become part of our everyday lives. This is a document to be lived, not simply read and discussed and then put on a shelf.

The Joy of the Gospel and Our Call to Joy

St. Francis of Assisi had a very clear understanding of the importance of the incarnation, of the Word of God becoming flesh in the person of Jesus of Nazareth. Because of this incarnation, humanity was redeemed, restored to its original harmony with God and with all of God's creation. The Gospels, the story of Jesus's life and ministry on earth, then became the primary and privileged place of encounter with the divine. In these four relatively brief accounts of what Jesus said and did, we can find the meaning and direction of our own lives. If we live according to these words, we will be sharing in God's plan for our world.

The more we let the word of God become part of our life, the more we will discover the joy that St. Francis experienced in living the Gospels. The more we conform our lives to the life of Christ, the more we will be moved by the presence and inspiration of the Holy Spirit. And the genius of the Gospels is that they reveal to us what St. Ignatius and the Jesuits articulated as "Finding God in all things."

Pope Francis, himself a Jesuit, seeks to help us understand the joy that St. Francis of Assisi and so many of the saints found as they lived the Gospels in their prayer, their reflection, and their life in the world. God created us for joyful union with him, here and hereafter. Our Christian call is a call to joy.

CHAPTER ONE

"WE HAVE FOUND THE MESSIAH"

Discovering Jesus in the Gospels

I
f joy is the keynote of Pope Francis's first major document, the song is that of the Gospels: "The joy of the Gospel fills the hearts and lives of all who encounter Jesus. Those who accept his offer of salvation are set free from sin, sorrow, inner emptiness and loneliness" (1). As Catholics, as Christians, we are followers of Jesus of Nazareth. And we encounter Jesus first and foremost in the Gospels, the stories of the first witnesses to God's incarnation. This was the starting point for the first Christians and it continues to be our starting point today. It is also the point to which we return any time our religious lives become too confused and chaotic.

St. Francis discovered this in the Middle Ages. As the pope, the bishops, and the Holy Roman Emperor were increasingly using religion as a means of achieving political power and economic success, this son of a merchant rejected worldly ambition and returned to the Gospels as a guide to daily life. Pope Francis is making sure that we know that we have to begin our evangelization with an encounter with Jesus in the Gospels. The essential message can be obscured by layers of abstract philosophy and theology. The truth of the Gospel is abandoned in favor of proof texts and moralizing.

To share the Good News, we need to first know the Good News ourselves. And we need to be sure that we hear it as good news. I'm still haunted by something a colleague said to me when I was first working in Catholic publishing. She said, "I don't think I've ever heard the good news preached." She was older than me, and her early experiences of the Church were in the 1950s, when more emphasis was placed on guilt, fear, and "thou shalt nots." She was also divorced after her husband left her and their children for another woman. But even knowing that background, I felt sad for her, because I had even at that time known more than one truly gifted preacher of the Gospel, and it had been a real source of encouragement and good news in my own life.

The Gospels and the Scriptures as a whole are a foundation to which we can return when we need to be reminded of God's encounter with the people he has chosen (and that includes all of us). I grew up reading the Bible in school, and as an English major in college I learned to read it along with the other works of great literature. Like any good book, the Bible speaks truth in a variety of ways, sometimes far more deeply than a book of facts and scientific proof. And the words of scripture in turn find their way into other literature. St. Jerome asserted, "Ignorance of Scripture is ignorance of Christ." To put a more positive spin on his words, if, knowledge of Scripture is knowledge of Christ, then any encounter with the words of the Bible is an opportunity to discover God in his word.

> Proclaiming Christ means showing that to believe in and to follow him is not only something right and true, but also something beautiful, capable of filling life with new splendour and profound joy, even in the midst of difficulties.

Every expression of true beauty can thus be acknowledged as a path leading to an encounter with the Lord Jesus. (167)

One of the great gifts of past centuries is that so many of the arts found patronage in the Church. Whether in painting or stained glass or music, the Word of God comes to life in so many ways beyond the written word. It doesn't even have to be great art. I think of the many times I've heard passages of Scripture in songs written for the liturgy in the decades since Vatican II. The music that has found a permanent place in our hymnals has lyrics drawn almost entirely from Scripture. We can dismiss the musical styles as dated or simplistic, but the words remain the words of Scripture, the Word of God.

One of the reasons I began writing about Scripture was that I knew that there must be a way to bring it into people's everyday lives. I never tire of the lectionary cycle. I hear new things in the Mass readings every Sunday, as though I've never heard them before. This is the wonder of the Gospel as a living revelation.

God's word is unpredictable in its power. The Gospel speaks of a seed which, once sown, grows by itself, even as the farmer sleeps (Mk 4:26–29). The Church has to accept this unruly freedom of the word, which accomplishes what it wills in ways that surpass our calculations and ways of thinking. (22)

One of the things that we need to remember is that we're preaching Jesus, not the institutional Church. It's easy to get caught up in the rules and regulations of the institution and forget that we are saved not by the Church but by the person of Jesus or the Church as the body of Christ. It is there we meet the person of Jesus and a community of children of God. But this ideal is sometimes not well represented on a daily basis. This is perhaps one of the strongest themes in the pope's document. He has spoken numerous times on the need to go out to where the people are. In a note to the bishops of Argentina, he said, "A church that doesn't get out, sooner or later, gets sick from being locked up.... It's also true that getting out in the street runs the risk of an accident, but frankly I prefer a church that has accidents a thousand times to a church that gets sick."

You can't give what you haven't got. But it doesn't take a lot. The Samaritan woman had a brief but meaningful conversation with Jesus at Jacob's well and then ran to tell the townspeople, "Come meet a man who told me everything I ever did." What had happened in that encounter? She felt listened to. She felt like she mattered. She felt like her experience, with all of its ups and downs, made a difference.

New Catholics evangelize differently than long time faithful. They have an excitement over the newness of their faith. Sometimes the people who they evangelize are those longtime Catholics. I'm always fascinated at the reasons people have for coming into the Church. The story of the Samaritan woman always reminds me of this enthusiasm for the faith we often see in new converts. Ideally this first burst of enthusiasm will be nourished and deepened through the years, as they grow in knowledge of the faith. Often these people become the core of ongoing RCIA groups in the parish. They are able to lead others along the path that they themselves have followed.

We need to realize that the pope is calling us to experience the joy of the Gospel for ourselves, not just as yet one more task to add to our already full to-do lists. And sometimes being able to take time out to remember how God touched our lives in the first place is the best thing we can do. There's a balance between going within and going forth. Pope Francis, who spends time in prayer daily, would be the first to acknowledge this. It's not about saying prayers or thinking holy thoughts. It's about being open to God, letting God touch us, letting God use us for his holy purposes. It's not about what we want; it's about what God wants.

This is not an idea new or unique to this pope. The best spiritual guides know that we can't keep going without taking time to replenish our energy. It's such a basic part of human life that it holds true in every aspect of who we are, from taking time for a healthy breakfast to remembering to stop for gas before setting out on a trip or taking time away from work for both vacation and professional enrichment. But how often do we forget or overlook any one of these things? Our spiritual life is no different.

If we're not joyful people, how can we expect people to want to share what we've discovered? This may have been less of an issue when most people took it for granted that they belonged to the religion of their parents, grandparents and distant ancestors. Many religious groups have an ethnic component that means one is literally born into a religious identity. Catholicism has had nearly that much of a blood tie for centuries. Whether you liked it or not, whether you believed everything the Church taught or not, you were Catholic. The farthest away you could get was "lapsed" or non-practicing Catholic. This is increasingly not the case in our century. People are increasingly mobile and increasingly secular. Religious affiliation becomes more of a choice, more of an adult decision. Many newcomers in the Catholic Church have been raised in homes with little or no religious background. Will people look at us and see that we have something attractive that's missing in their own lives? Will they see that our religious identity gives us a sense of meaning and purpose in the often difficult struggles of daily life? If not, then evangelization is going to be a fruitless and futile task.

Pope Francis makes this point quite clearly at the beginning of his exhortation: "For if we have received the love which restores meaning to our lives, how can we fail to share that love with others?" (8) The key, then, is knowing and believing that we have experienced this love of God in our lives, that we have found meaning through our belief in the life, death, and resurrection of Jesus. Whether we are cradle Catholics, have joined the Church as adults, or have moved in and out of belief throughout our lives, we need to return again and again to this central encounter with Jesus Christ.

Theologians speak of the *kerygma,* a Greek word that means preaching. This is the first and most essential proclamation of the Christian faith. This is the "mystery of faith" that we proclaim in the center of the Eucharist: "Christ has died, Christ is risen, Christ will come again." The pope fleshes out the centrality of this teaching in this way:

> On the lips of the catechist the first proclamation must ring out over and over: "Jesus Christ loves you; he gave his life to save you; and now he is living at your side every day to enlighten, strengthen and free you." This first proclamation is called "first" not because it exists at the beginning and can then be forgotten or replaced by other more important things. It is first in a qualitative sense because it is the principal proclamation, the one which we must hear again and again in different ways, the one which we must announce one way or another throughout the process of catechesis, at every level and moment (126).

When we forget why we believe what we believe, when we get bogged down in controversies and theories and abstract theological discussions, when we get distracted by the ordinary concerns of daily life, this is the central message that brings us back to the core of our faith and helps us once again to get our priorities straight. If we have been saved and sustained by a love so deep that death itself couldn't destroy it, then that love will see us through whatever darkness we are experiencing in our lives.

Our Catholic faith, like the Jewish faith out of which it grew, depends heavily on memory. It is in our own past experience of God, but also the experience of those who have gone before us in faith, that we find the meaning and the strength to live fully in the present and push forward into the future. The Jewish celebration of Passover commemorates the central saving experience when God delivered the Hebrews from their Egyptian oppressors. From that day to this, the Jewish people gather to tell the story and enact the ritual of that salvation. In a similar way, we gather at Easter to celebrate the passover of Jesus from death to new life. Those saving acts are made present and active once again in the celebration. This active remembrance is part of every Mass. And it's no less a part of the personal experience of each and every one of us.

> The apostles never forgot the moment when Jesus touched their hearts: "It was about four o'clock in the afternoon" (Jn 1:39). Together with Jesus, this remembrance makes present to us "a great cloud of witnesses" (Heb 12:1), some of whom, as believers, we recall with great joy: "Remember your leaders, those who spoke to you the word of God" (Heb 13:7). Some of them were ordinary people who were close to us and introduced us to the life of faith: "I am reminded of your sincere faith, a faith that dwelt first in your grandmother Lois and your mother Eunice" (2 Tim 1:5). The believer is essentially "one who remembers." (13)

Each of us can most likely point to one or more times in our lives when we had a deeply personal experience of God, when we made a decision to claim the faith that someone else had presented to us. What we will probably discover about this memory is that it was less of a lightning bolt than a steady spring rain watering and breaking open seeds that had been planted long before. This will help us to take a gradual approach to sharing the Good News with people we meet. We don't need to expect instant results or a dramatic conversion experience. Jesus and the apostles moved throughout the countryside speaking about the kingdom of God. Some people followed them immediately, while others may have needed time to think about the message and let it take root in their lives. But at some point they would have remembered a word, a phrase, perhaps even just a loving look from the Lord, and at that moment the pieces of the puzzle clicked into place.

Pope Francis shows a deep understanding of how this gradual call to conversion takes place in our encounters with one another. At the heart of it is an openness to what's happening in the lives of the people we meet. Too often we forget that people are nearly always dealing with a whole range of issues, experiences, and emotions that may not be obvious in our casual, day-to-day encounters. While we might think that we have the solution to their problems and even believe—based on our own genuine experience and conviction—that Jesus is the answer, beginning there will be both counterproductive and disrespectful of the way God works in the lives of his creatures. Rather than overwhelming others with one more decision to make, one more thing to think about, we need to begin simply by being present to them and listening to their concerns:

In this preaching, which is always respectful and gentle, the first step is personal dialogue, when the other person speaks and shares his or her joys, hopes and concerns for loved ones, or so many other heartfelt needs. Only afterwards is it possible to bring up God's word, perhaps by reading a Bible verse or relating a story, but always keeping in mind the fundamental message: the personal love of God who became man, who gave himself up for us, who is living and who offers us his salvation and his friendship. (126)

The best way to learn to do this well is to be constantly aware that it is God working through us, not our own efforts, that will touch the hearts and lives of the people we meet. We need to remember our own experience of conversion. We need to live our lives in such a way that God's love shines through us. And sometimes we simply need to get out of the way and let God work.

Joy in Action
Spend time getting acquainted (or reacquainted) with the Scriptures. The readings for Sunday Mass are a perfect place to start. You won't be sidetracked by some of the more obscure passages in the Bible. These readings have been carefully selected. All of the Gospels are covered. Significant parts of the Old Testament, Paul's letters and other key passages in the New Testament are included. Commentaries are readily available. Check your parish bulletin, find an online resource, read the passages before Mass and then pay attention when they're read. Look at them again after Mass. Pick out one line to ponder through the week.

Read one of the Gospels from beginning to end, at one sitting if possible. The Gospel of Mark is a good place to start.

Experiment with the Ignatian practice of putting yourself in a Gospel scene in your imagination. You might imagine how you would react to Jesus's words in John 1:39, "Come and see," or how you would respond to his question in Luke 9:18, "Who do people say that I am?" Listening to Scripture is another good way to become more familiar with the word of God. Find an audio version on CD or MP3 that you can listen to during your commute or workout. You might also want to try different translations (ask your local Catholic bookseller for help) to find the one that most resonates with you.

You might want to try a modern retelling of the story of Jesus. Author Joseph Girzone's *Stories of Jesus* is a popular treatment and the miniseries *Jesus of Nazareth* is widely available on DVD and streaming video. Keep in mind that some authors often indulge in imaginative recreations. Check their interpretation against the Gospels if something seems unusual or not quite right.

CHAPTER TWO

"MUD ON OUR SHOES"
The Church Meets the Real World

As much as we might want to see the Church as some other worldly city of God, set high on a hill as an example of perfection and holiness, we know that's not the case. The Church exists in the world and is all too often tainted by the same temptations to power, riches, and prestige that so often lead to scandal and disaster in secular society. This is not something new to our generation. It has existed as long as we've had recorded history and probably long before that. The sooner we accept this reality, the sooner we can get on with the task of sharing the joy that the Gospel can bring into our everyday lives in that same real world.

We see then that the task of evangelization operates within the limits of language and of circumstances. It constantly seeks to communicate more effectively the truth of the Gospel in a specific context, without renouncing the truth, the goodness and the light which it can bring whenever perfection is not possible. A missionary heart is aware of these limits and makes itself "weak with the weak...everything for everyone" (1 Cor 9:22). It never closes itself off, never retreats into its own security, never opts for rigidity and defensiveness. It realizes that it has to grow in its own understanding of the Gospel and in discerning the paths of the Spirit, and so it always does what good it can, even if in the process, its shoes get soiled by the mud of the street. (45)

Two dangers here are to pretend that the Church as an institution is perfect and preserved from human failings or to see only the scandals and imperfections and lose sight of the fact that the Holy Spirit is still guiding the Church. If we take a realistic approach to the Church and its place in the world, we can see a path forward through the sometimes overwhelming storms that arise: the clergy sex abuse crisis, the improprieties of the Vatican bank, the collusion between Church leaders and oppressive governments, the opulent lifestyles of some of the hierarchy, and the garden variety hypocrisy that can creep into local parish organizations. We all have individual weakness and failings. A Church made up of human beings will have a similar collection of the same problems. But we believe that God's grace can help both the individuals and the institutions to find new possibilities.

If we adopt a humble attitude toward both ourselves and the world, we will be able to see more goodness than evil, more peace than conflict, more grace than sin. In that fertile ground the seeds of the Gospel can find nourishment and grow. Pope Francis reminds us that people are far more likely to be looking at our lives than listening to our words: "We need to remember that all religious teaching ultimately has to be reflected in the teacher's way of life, which awakens the assent of the heart by its nearness, love and witness." His own example from the time of his election has been one of the most powerful means of drawing people to take another look at the Catholic Church.

St. Francis advised his followers to make their lives the heart of their preaching. This is often phrased as, "Preach the Gospel at all times. If necessary use words." Any parent knows that children are far more likely to pick up on what we do than simply what we say. If we have truly experienced God's love, then we will act accordingly more often than not. If we have known God's mercy and forgiveness, we will extend that mercy to others. If we acknowledge our need for reconciliation and improvement, we will be more patient with the failings of others. If we admit that there are places where the institutional Church needs to be converted and transformed, we will better be able to call secular institutions to conversion. No one listens willingly to someone who speaks to them from a position of self-righteousness and judgment. Again and again in the Gospels, Jesus reserves his harshest words for those who ignore their own weakness in order to lord it over others.

Pope Francis has been quick to admit both his own failings as well as the weaknesses that beset the present-day institutional Church. It's much easier to point to mistakes that the Church has made in the distant past than to acknowledge the faults of the present—and then take action to amend those faults. While the action might not be as quick as some might hope, there have been real signs of conversion in the way the Church is being governed. One of Francis's first acts as pope was to hold a meeting with all of the journalists present in Rome for the conclave and papal election. His engaging talk with them and his respect for the work that they did was the first indication that he was willing to be more direct in his dealings with the media than the more retiring Pope Benedict. Indeed, the Vatican press office has more than once found itself nuancing something Pope Francis has said in an interview or press conference, but this hasn't stopped the pope from continuing to speak to the media directly.

But even when one is making repairs and improvements, all the energy can't be focused solely on internal affairs. One of the main themes of Pope Francis's writing and preaching has been the need to go out into the world. He has framed the task of evangelization less as a way of growing the membership list and more as a way of taking the Good News to those who most need to hear it. This isn't about using the same methods that have been tried in the past with mixed or even disappointing results.

> When we adopt a pastoral goal and a missionary style which would actually reach everyone without exception or exclusion, the message has to concentrate on the essentials, on what is most beautiful, most grand, most appealing and at the same time most necessary. The message is simplified, while losing none of its depth and truth, and thus becomes all the more forceful and convincing. (35)

As we have already seen, love, mercy, and compassion are the keys to this simple message. Openness and transparency are increasingly part of the governance of the Church, although we still have a long way to go. Whether deserved or not, the Vatican has a reputation of secret and mysterious operations. Pope Francis is doing his best to change the impression but also the reality. The political and business machinery of the Church can no longer cloak itself in the divine mysteries of the spiritual reality. We can hope that this will free the spiritual task of evangelization from some of its human entanglements, making it once again an attractive and compelling message.

Talking about Religion

We've all heard the saying that politics and religion are not appropriate topics for polite conversation. We might do well to heed this in these days of rampant social media and 24/7 cable news and talk shows. And we've probably all felt accosted at times by "religious" messages that were thinly disguised diatribes about the evils of society or our own personal failings. The rancor and vitriol that accompany too much of what passes for religious (and political) discourse today might be one of the biggest obstacles in preaching a genuine call to experience God's plan for our lives.

In The Joy of the Gospel, Pope Francis issues a refreshing call: "I invite everyone to be bold and creative in this task of rethinking the goals, structures, style and methods of evangelization in their respective communities." When we think about evangelization, it might help to take it out of a religious context to get a better grasp of what's being called for here.

Each of us has one or more things we're passionate about—a sport, a hobby, a place, a person. We talk about these things with enthusiasm and in fairly extensive detail. We're happy to share our knowledge with friends and acquaintances, sometimes even with strangers on the street. We find groups either in real life or online who share our commitment and our passion. It almost never occurs to us that people might be offended by what we share. And rarely do we try overtly to get others to adopt our interests. We're thrilled when someone else discovers the same activity and our joy is shared and multiplied.

What if we could find a way to share our faith in a similar way? We wouldn't worry about offending people because we would simply be sharing our own joy in God's love. We could quote a passage from Scripture as a way to offer comfort and inspiration rather than as a way of proving a debate point. We could be content with planting seeds. And we could leave some freedom for others to share our interests or not, believing all the while that the Spirit has the greater task.

One of the drawbacks in the Church's work of evangelization has been an attitude that says, "We have all the answers and everything is certain." This may have seemed effective in the past, although it didn't play well among people of other faiths. In the fifty years since the Second Vatican Council, the Church has been moving back and forth along these lines, balancing a healthy questioning with a need for a clear message; a conviction of absolute truth with an awareness of past mistakes. Pope Francis is bringing the openness of the Council to the forefront once again:

> The Church is herself a missionary disciple; she needs to grow in her interpretation of the revealed word and in her understanding of truth.... For those who long for a mono-lithic body of doctrine guarded by all and leaving no room for nuance, this might appear as undesirable and leading to confusion. But in fact such variety serves to bring out and develop different facets of the inexhaustible riches of the Gospel. (40)

If we are truly convinced of the truth of the Gospel, the truth of God's revelation held in trust by the Church to be shared with the world, then we can find ways of presenting that message without making others feel belittled or condemned. The world in which we live has a great deal of diversity. The presence of other faiths, some older than Christianity and several sharing the same roots, is a reality in our world that is not going to go away in the foreseeable future. To engage these people in an adversarial relationship will do more harm than good. But if we begin with the beliefs and convictions that we hold in common, we can find ways to share the richness of our own faith and in turn be enriched by insights that others have grasped.

Again and again Pope Francis reminds us that we're to go out to meet people where they are, not wait for them to come to church. While he would be the first to remind us that the Eucharist is the source and summit of the Christian life, he also knows that sometimes it's a long journey to get there. And we can't wait at the top while people struggle on the way up. We need to join them on the journey. We need to bring Christ to them on the way.

> A Church which "goes forth" is a Church whose doors are open. Going out to others in order to reach the fringes of humanity does not mean rushing out aimlessly into the world. Often it is better simply to slow down, to put aside our eagerness in order to see and listen to others, to stop rushing from one thing to another and to remain with someone who has faltered along the way. (46)

Too often evangelization programs are all about getting people through the doors of the parish church. But we can't always guarantee that what they will see and hear when they get there will make them want to return. What works for one person may not work for someone else. What we need to do is make sure that people hear the really essential message, the message of the Good News. The person they need to meet is Jesus Christ. If that happens in our parish church, we should consider ourselves blessed. If it doesn't, then we need to take a good look at what can be changed so that people truly feel welcomed and loved.

The pope makes a somewhat radical suggestion that opening the doors of the Church isn't just a pretty metaphor: "One concrete sign of such openness is that our church doors should always be open, so that if someone, moved by the Spirit, comes there looking for God, he or she will not find a closed door" (47). This is something that people (and parish councils) will argue about endlessly, but it can't be denied as an ideal, whatever the practical complications. In some cities, churches have found ways to open their doors to the homeless during the cold winter months, offering them a warm place to sleep. Many churches have food pantries and soup kitchens to meet the physical needs of their neighbors, but have yet to find ways to be open to the spiritual needs of those who might wander in during the day.

Just as challenging are the pope's words about the sacraments, those "doors to the sacred":

> There are other doors that should not be closed either. Everyone can share in some way in the life of the Church; everyone can be part of the community, nor should the doors of the sacraments be closed for simply any reason. This is especially true of the sacrament which is itself "the door": baptism. The Eucharist, although it is the fullness of sacramental life, is not a prize for the perfect but a powerful medicine and nourishment for the weak. These convictions have pastoral consequences that we are called to consider with prudence and boldness. Frequently, we act as arbiters of grace rather than its facilitators. But the Church is not a tollhouse; it is the house of the Father, where there is a place for everyone, with all their problems. (51)

Some of the first stories that emerged about Cardinal Bergoglio had to do with his emphasis that baptism not be denied to children of single mothers. The story was told of a woman who had approached numerous priests to have her child baptized and was turned away because she wasn't married. This was one clear example of the need to emphasize God's mercy over judgment. There has been talk in the past year of finding new ways of working with those who are divorced and remarried in order to alleviate some of their feelings of exclusion at being denied communion. This is where Pope Francis's long years of pastoral experience shine through the sometimes obscure theological disputes that can surround these issues.

Perhaps the most difficult sacrament in the minds of many Catholics, both faithful and lapsed, is that of confession. The ambiguity surrounding this sacrament is perhaps suggested by the variety of names it bears: penance, confession, reconciliation. Pope Francis has made it clear that the emphasis is on mercy and forgiveness. In The Joy of the Gospel, he writes:

> I want to remind priests that the confessional must not be a torture chamber but rather an encounter with the Lord's mercy which spurs us on to do our best. A small step, in the midst of great human limitations, can be more pleasing to God than a life which appears outwardly in order but moves through the day without confronting great difficulties. Everyone needs to be touched by the comfort and attraction of God's saving love, which is mysteriously at work in each person, above and beyond their faults and failings. (44)

Like his predecessors, the pope has himself publicly celebrated the sacrament of reconciliation, as both priest and penitent. During the 2014 Lenten season, he paused before hearing confessions to make his own confession. The photos and video were quickly shared in the news and social media. He never misses an opportunity to lead by example, and people are beginning to pay attention.

The Action of the Church in the World

The pope, as the leader of the universal Church, is often the face of the Church to the rest of the world. Bishops and cardinals, especially in the United States, have taken to themselves the task of being the voice of the Church, proclaiming the Church's teachings on various moral doctrines. But The Joy of the Gospel reiterates the teaching of Vatican II that the bulk of the Church's mission to the secular world is to be carried out by laypeople, ordinary faithful Catholics who let the message of the Gospel inform their activities in the world. This is both a privilege and a challenge, as the pope makes clear:

> Lay people are, put simply, the vast majority of the People of God. The minority—ordained ministers—are at their service. There has been a growing awareness of the identity and mission of the laity in the Church…. Even if many are now involved in the lay ministries, this involvement is not reflected in a greater penetration of Christian values in the social, political and economic sectors. It often remains tied to tasks within the Church, without a real commitment to applying the Gospel to the transformation of society. The formation of the laity and the evangelization of professional and intellectual life represent a significant pastoral challenge (102).

The distinction the pope makes here is one also made by Vatican II. While various ministries in the Church are more open to laypeople, the place where the laity are most needed is in the everyday life of society: politics, business, the economy, the home, the neighborhood. Through the example and witness of ordinary Catholics, the message of the Gospel finds its way into all aspects of life, not just the Sunday liturgy and the internal workings of the Church. This is in keeping with Pope Francis's insistence that the Church cannot survive if it turns in on itself.

This is also clear in what he says about the specific role of women. Here he acknowledges that the male-dominated governing structures of the Church will benefit from the perspective and involvement of women.

The Church acknowledges the indispensable contribution which women make to society through the sensitivity, intuition and other distinctive skill sets which they, more than men, tend to possess. I think, for example, of the special concern which women show to others, which finds a particular, even if not exclusive, expression in motherhood. I readily acknowledge that many women share pastoral responsibilities with priests, helping to guide people, families and groups and offering new contributions to theological reflection. But we need to create still broader opportunities for a more incisive female presence in the Church. (103)

He has recently appointed several women to the Pontifical Council for the Protection of Minors, a special group of advisors selected to deal with the clergy sex abuse crisis. More appointments will most likely follow. While he has again said that the ordination of women is not a valid direction for the Church, he seems to recognize the need for alternative roles for women in the Church so that their unique perspective is not lost.

Just as he consistently cautions Vatican professionals, most of them clergy, about avoiding the temptations of power and "careerism," so he wants to be sure that the laity's role in the Church doesn't end up creating a subset of Church professionals more concerned with their own advancement than with the spread of the Gospel. This will always be a complex issue, but it's easier for laypeople to wrestle with their role when it's presented as distinct and valuable in the life of the Church, and when efforts are also made to discourage the rise of a superior "clerical class."

Joy in Action

Think about the people with whom you interact every day. What are they most concerned about? What might they struggle with? What sense do you have of whether they're religious or not? Is this something that you talk about with them? Could you?

How might you take Pope Francis's words to heart and put them into practice in some small way?

CHAPTER THREE

"ALL ARE WELCOME"

Gathering with Others as a Community of Faith

The Catholic Church has always struck a balance between solitude and community. Depending on our personalities, some of us may tend more toward one side or the other. But both are needed for a healthy spiritual life. Functioning as a local community is another of the many ways the Church finds its way in the real world.

Finding a parish community that meets your spiritual needs can be a challenge. Like a family, the parish is one's spiritual home, but it may not always be as comforting or nurturing as one might wish. Historically and canonically, people belong to a parish that is located in the same geographical location as their home. This can be challenging at times, but it can also keep us from gathering only with like-minded individuals. Learning to get along with all kinds of people and listening patiently to a wide variety of opinions can encourage us to grow in all manner of virtues, including patience, tolerance, and even love of enemies!

The parish is not an outdated institution; precisely because it possesses great flexibility, it can assume quite different contours depending on the openness and missionary creativity of the pastor and the community.... This presumes that it really is in contact with the homes and the lives of its people, and does not become a useless structure out of touch with people or a self-absorbed cluster made up of a chosen few.... It is a community of communities, a sanctuary where the thirsty come to drink in the midst of their journey, and a centre of constant missionary outreach. We must admit, though, that the call to review and renew our parishes has not yet sufficed to bring them nearer to people, to make them environments of living communion and participation, and to make them completely mission-oriented. (28)

A small group gathering can provide an alternative to one's parish home, a place both more intimate and more reflective. It doesn't replace the parish but it offers another kind of accountability.

Pope Francis offers encouragement and inspiration in the sometimes daunting task of gathering with others. One of his reasons for living in the St. Martha guest house instead of in the more secluded papal apartments was because he recognized in himself the need for a regular community gathering. Many of us may have the same need. And even those of us who prefer solitude can recognize an accountability and even joy in regular gatherings.

Today, when the networks and means of human communication have made unprecedented advances, we sense the challenge of finding and sharing a "mystique" of living together, of mingling and encounter, of embracing and supporting one another, of stepping into this flood tide which, while chaotic, can become a genuine experience of fraternity, a caravan of solidarity, a sacred pilgrimage. (87)

Evangelization is always a two-way street. We might think that we're the ones with the message, with the answers, with the Good News, and yet time and time again we discover that we learn as much from the people we're with as we had when we began the conversation. One of the problems we often have in our professional and social gatherings is a lack of diversity. We have fewer and fewer opportunities to interact with people of different ages, ethnic backgrounds, and religious leanings. One of the things Pope Francis specifically encourages is keeping both the elderly and young people in all of our faith conversations:

> Whenever we attempt to read the signs of the times it is helpful to listen to young people and the elderly. Both represent a source of hope for every people. The elderly bring with them memory and the wisdom of experience, which warns us not to foolishly repeat our past mistakes. Young people call us to renewed and expansive hope, for they represent new directions for humanity and open us up to the future, lest we cling to a nostalgia for structures and customs which are no longer life-giving in today's world. (108)

One of the most exciting things about Pope Francis's papacy is that he creates talking points almost daily. Finally there's some good news about the Church in the news. We can share a line or two from one of his homilies or a photo from Vatican Square with our Facebook friends. I have many people in my circle of friends and acquaintances who hold a variety of religious viewpoints (or who avoid religion altogether). Sometimes I like to offer a range of prayerful thoughts and ideas. "Let those who have ears to hear, hear."

Pope Francis is a marvelous example of someone who is clear about what he believes and what he stands for without making people feel judged or rejected. And he has said many times that the core of the Gospel message is that God loves each and every person, no matter who they are or what they have or haven't done. God isn't waiting for them to be good before he loves them. He simply loves. This can't be overstated.

> The centrality of the kerygma calls for stressing those elements which are most needed today: it has to express God's saving love which precedes any moral and religious obligation on our part; it should not impose the truth but appeal to freedom; it should be marked by joy, encouragement, liveliness and a harmonious balance which will not reduce preaching to a few doctrines which are at times more philosophical than evangelical. All this demands on the part of the evangelizer certain attitudes which foster openness to the message: approachability, readiness for dialogue, patience, a warmth and welcome which is non-judgmental. (165)

Pope Francis has found a hearing in some unlikely places in these first months of his papacy. People seem to be willing to listen to what he has to say, even if they don't agree. At times this raises perhaps unrealistic expectations of change, and many observers in the media have noted that people are bound to be disappointed when those expectations aren't met. But then Pope Francis follows a man who was also frequently misunderstood, so he's probably not unduly concerned about that.

There's an openness about Pope Francis that carries a great degree of genuineness and authenticity. He is clearly a man of prayer, a humble man, a sincere man. It's not so much a back-slapping bonhomie, a "hey I'm just one of the guys" so much as it's a sense of someone who cares deeply about people. He has stepped into being pastor to the whole world and it seems to fit. He is perfectly comfortable talking to ordinary people, often about the things that they struggle with in their lives.

He never forgets that there are real people at the heart of every struggle. It can be tempting to reduce complex issues to academic debates, slogans, and shouting matches. Pope Francis reminds us to set aside the rhetoric and remember that people on both sides of any issue are children of God. He doesn't discount the very real presence of evil in the world, but he recognizes that too often those whom we demonize are actually deeply troubled human beings desperate for understanding, compassion, and mercy. And sometimes those people are ourselves.

Pope Francis has made it very clear that he knows his own faults and failings, the mistakes he has made in the past and the temptations he still struggles with. This isn't some kind of artificial piety for him. It's quite real. And so he's able to take to heart the words of the Gospel that tell us not to judge. When Jesus said, "Let the one among you who is without sin cast the first stone," he was speaking to the religious leaders of the day. He must have wondered whether their self-righteousness would extend that far.

Joy in Action

Are you more comfortable in a small faith-sharing group or a large parish gathering? How might you take a few steps beyond that comfort zone to try different ways of gathering with others?

How difficult is it for you to find a balance between private and public prayer, between action and contemplation? What can you do to find people who can support you in your efforts to live a life that is growing ever more faithful to the Gospel?

How does having a group of fellow Christians keep you accountable?

CHAPTER FOUR

"DON'T LET THE DEVIL STEAL YOUR JOY"
Overcoming Obstacles and Resistance

The section of The Joy of the Gospel that generated the greatest buzz when the document was released had to do with both the internal struggles of the Church and comments on the economic realities in the world. This shouldn't surprise us given the media's penchant for focusing on division and conflict. If their argument would be that it's what sells the news, then we need to look to ourselves. Are we inordinately interested in competition and division? This attitude might be at the heart of the greatest challenge we face in bringing the Good News to those who need to hear it. If we can't get along among ourselves, what kind of message are we presenting to the world?

Pope Francis stands in a long line of prophets, including Jesus himself, when he calls both society and the Church to task for their failures to live out the message of the Gospel. No one escapes his challenging words here. In much the same way that we try to explain away the difficult passages in the Gospels by saying that Jesus doesn't mean what he seems to be saying, so people on both sides of the political spectrum were quick to point out that the pope didn't mean to criticize them (or their political and financial allies).

Exclusion, apathy, complacency, worldliness: These are the faults that the pope sees as standing in the way of us going forth and sharing the Good News. As an antidote, he holds forth the importance of listening, inclusion, community, and sacrifice. And ultimately his answer is to hold on to the joy of the Gospel and the joy of sharing that Good News.

Pope Francis isn't wringing his hands here about how awful the secular world is or even how sinful parts of the Church can be. He's taking a realistic stance, not a defensive one. He's working to meet sinfulness with grace and forgiveness, not judgment and an air of certainty that says we have all the answers if the world would only listen to us. We don't have all the answers. Only God does. What the pope is doing here is confronting us with the results of our sin and asking, "What are we going to do about this? How are we going to get better?"

> It never closes itself off, never retreats into its own security, never opts for rigidity and defensiveness. It realizes that it has to grow in its own understanding of the Gospel and in discerning the paths of the Spirit, and so it always does what good it can, even if in the process, its shoes get soiled by the mud of the street. (45)

The pope is not naive in his approach to the world. He readily acknowledges (and confronts) the sinfulness and the evil that exist in the world. Like any true prophet, he challenges sinners to repent. In Buenos Aires he challenged the military dictatorship that threatened his slum priests. In Rome he has challenged the Italian mafia. He understands the reality on the streets of our cities better than almost any pope in recent history, and probably better than many bishops and priests. When he writes, "The joy of living frequently fades, lack of respect for others and violence are on the rise, and inequality is increasingly evident. It is a struggle to live and, often, to live with precious little dignity" (52), we know that he has seen this for himself. Nor is he content to talk about evil as an abstract concept or as something we find only in the world of organized crime and political oppression. He brings it home in clear and concrete examples that make all of us cringe a bit:

> How can it be that it is not a news item when an elderly homeless person dies of exposure, but it is news when the stock market loses two points? This is a case of exclusion. Can we continue to stand by when food is thrown away while people are starving? This is a case of inequality. (53)

> Almost without being aware of it, we end up being incapable of feeling compassion at the outcry of the poor, weeping for other people's pain, and feeling a need to help them, as though all this were someone else's responsibility and not our own. The culture of prosperity deadens us; we are thrilled if the market offers us something new to purchase; and in the meantime all those lives stunted for lack of opportunity seem a mere spectacle; they fail to move us. (54)

Not one to dwell overmuch on the problems in the world, Pope Francis has a way of looking at the challenges and obstacles being presented and finding a way to turn them into opportunities. He doesn't do this with a naive optimism but rather out of years of experience with what works in the task of evangelization. Where others might see only the difficulties of big cities, he sees a unique way for people to connect with one another and form new communities of faith:

What is called for is an evangelization capable of shedding light on these new ways of relating to God, to others and to the world around us, and inspiring essential values. It must reach the places where new narratives and paradigms are being formed, bringing the word of Jesus to the inmost soul of our cities. Cities are multicultural; in the larger cities, a connective network is found in which groups of people share a common imagination and dreams about life, and new human interactions arise, new cultures, invisible cities. (74)

This passage expresses a hope-filled challenge to take the story of the Gospels, the experience of a small group of rural fishermen and villages in Palestine over two thousand years ago, and make it relevant and inspiring to a world that is much different on the outside but remarkably similar in the minds and hearts of its citizens. This is why the parables and other stories in the Gospels continue to speak to us of God's care. As we find new ways of expressing this message, we will be enriched in unimaginable ways.

The Church in a Variety of Cultures
Francis is the first pope from the Americas, the first non-European pope in over eight hundred years. He understands that the Roman and European court customs that have become part of the dress and decoration of the Church and its liturgies over the years are not essential to the core message of the Gospel. It may have taken someone who has lived and ministered in another culture for his entire career to recognize this so deeply. It's easy to cling to the familiar, while denying other people the same cultural comfort.

Understanding the liturgy anew through the lens of another culture has been taking place for centuries, even millennia. As soon as the

Church moved out of Jerusalem and then beyond Rome, the shape of the liturgy has shifted and changed according to the styles and fashions of the surrounding culture. Some of this change was halted in response to the Reformation. But the movement of missionaries throughout the world ensured that while some traditions were frozen in place, others continued to adapt to local custom. Pope Francis, as a member of a missionary order and a citizen of a part of the world outside Europe, may have a much-needed perspective on this tension, as well as a willingness to take a fresh look:

> We would not do justice to the logic of the incarnation if we thought of Christianity as monocultural and monotonous. While it is true that some cultures have been closely associated with the preaching of the Gospel and the development of Christian thought, the revealed message is not identified with any of them; its content is transcultural. Hence in the evangelization of new cultures, or cultures which have not received the Christian message, it is not essential to impose a specific cultural form, no matter how beautiful or ancient it may be, together with the Gospel. The message that we proclaim always has a certain cultural dress, but we in the Church can sometimes fall into a needless hallowing of our own culture, and thus show more fanaticism than true evangelizing zeal. (117)

Sometimes these cultural expressions are somewhat superficial. Music and dance at liturgical celebrations often reflects the culture of the community. In Wisconsin, where I grew up, Mass accompanied by a polka band was a common occurrence. In Hispanic communities one might hear a mariachi band. But less obvious attitudes also become part of the rich meaning of the Church's traditions. As the Church continues the Pentecost mission of speaking to people in their own languages, the Gospel will find new paths into all cultures. We are familiar with cultural differences along ethnic lines, but we don't often think of the cultural differences that occur within a particular society, often along class and education lines. Pope Francis has continued his predecessors' openness to science and the academic worlds.

> Proclaiming the Gospel message to different cultures also involves proclaiming it to professional, scientific and academic circles. This means an encounter between faith, reason and the sciences with a view to developing new approaches and arguments on the issue of credibility, a creative apologetics which would encourage greater openness to the Gospel on the part of all. When certain categories of reason and the sciences are taken up into the proclamation of the message, these categories then become tools of evangelization; water is changed into wine. Whatever is taken up is not just redeemed, but becomes an instrument of the Spirit for enlightening and renewing the world. (132)

The Catholic Church is still apologizing for its mistake over Galileo and the sun. This can cause us to be lumped together with more fundamentalist Christian groups who deny any of the advances of science that call into question a literal interpretation of the Bible. But Catholicism has long been a proponent of scientific discovery. Learning to communicate with scientists and academics on their own ground is yet another way to bring the message of the Gospel into conversation with a world that needs to hear it. This requires a complex blend of confidence and humility, of knowing the truth of one's own beliefs and being open to the expertise of others.

The Challenge of the Institutional Church

The pope seems to recognize that all too often the institutional Church can be its own worst enemy in the call to go forth and proclaim the Good News of salvation. He recognizes that appearances matter. He knows that we need to live the truth we proclaim.

Let us go forth, then, let us go forth to offer everyone the life of Jesus Christ. Here I repeat for the entire Church what I have often said to the priests and laity of Buenos Aires: I prefer a Church which is bruised, hurting and dirty because it has been out on the streets, rather than a Church which is unhealthy from being confined and from clinging to its own security. I do not want a Church concerned with being at the centre and then ends by being caught up in a web of obsessions and procedures. If something should rightly disturb us and trouble our consciences, it is the fact that so many of our brothers and sisters are living without the strength, light and consolation born of friendship with Jesus Christ, without a community of faith to support them, without meaning and a goal in life. More than by fear of going astray, my hope is that we will be moved by the fear of remaining shut up within structures which give us a false sense of security, within rules which make us harsh judges, within habits which make us feel safe, while at our door people are starving and Jesus does not tire of saying to us: "Give them something to eat" (Mk 6:37). (49)

So many of his actions have deliberately carried a symbolic significance. Like Ezekiel and Jeremiah in the Hebrew Scriptures, he has been a living parable of humility, of openness, of God's love for all. Just weeks after his election, as the Church entered into the celebration of Holy Week, he celebrated the Holy Thursday liturgy not in the Basilica of St. John Lateran but in a juvenile detention facility. He washed the feet of twelve young offenders, male and female, Christian and Muslim, instead of twelve priests representing the first twelve apostles. In doing so he took the command of Jesus ("As I have done for you, so you must do for one another") out into the world where it gave real hope to those who needed to hear a message of acceptance. It may have finally silenced the somewhat petty internal disputes over whose feet can be washed that take place in chanceries and on liturgy committees and in the Wild West atmosphere of the Internet.

Through actions that seem to come quite naturally to this pope, he has made it quite apparent that other people, by contrast, are communicating a much different message, one that isn't always what Jesus may have intended. We may never know whether this is his intention or whether he is simply living the Gospel he has experienced with ever deepening authenticity. But people are beginning to recognize the difference these actions are making and the message behind them. When a cardinal or bishop is taken to task by the media for living ostentatiously, people are able to go beyond simple outrage and say, "This isn't the way to live the Gospel." And they can point to the example of Pope Francis to make their point.

Like his namesake St. Francis before him, the pope is making news because he's living Jesus's words in ways that too many people, many of them religious men and women, have said is impractical and perhaps even impossible.

Before all else, the Gospel invites us to respond to the God of love who saves us, to see God in others and to go forth from ourselves to seek the good of others. Under no circumstance can this invitation be obscured! All of the virtues are at the service of this response of love. If this invitation does not radiate forcefully and attractively, the edifice of the Church's moral teaching risks becoming a house of cards, and this is our greatest risk. It would mean that it is not the Gospel which is being preached, but certain doctrinal or moral points based on specific ideological options. The message will run the risk of losing its freshness and will cease to have "the fragrance of the Gospel." (39)

Pope Francis recognizes his own weaknesses and failings. He is able to live transparently.. He's not trying to keep up some sort of image of perfect holiness. And because he has been so much in the news, people are watching for the next thing he's going to do. It's not easy to live in the limelight, as many celebrities have discovered. But Pope Francis seems to be enjoying it, not because he's seeking attention but because he's comfortable with who he is. And he knows that the message is not how great he is but how great God is.

He doesn't let anyone off the hook. It's easy to point fingers at professionals in the Church, but the problems he talks about can apply just as well to us when we drag ourselves reluctantly to Church on Sunday morning (or stay home to catch up on sleep or laundry) because we've lost a sense of why we celebrate the Eucharist. And we've all had times when we've failed to identify ourselves as Catholic for fear of being thought naive, simple, or superstitious. Sometimes I just don't want to deal with people's questions and criticisms, often based on misunderstandings or misinterpretations of what's going on in the news. And yet, those can be some of the best opportunities for evangelization.

Pope Francis reminds us of how easy it is to forget why we do the things we do. And he knows that professional religious people are as susceptible to this failing as the most secular of business people and politicians. He refers to it as a "practical relativism."

> This practical relativism consists in acting as if God did not exist, making decisions as if the poor did not exist, setting goals as if others did not exist, working as if people who have not received the Gospel did not exist. It is striking that even some who clearly have solid doctrinal and spiritual convictions frequently fall into a lifestyle which leads to an attachment to financial security, or to a desire for power or human glory at all cost, rather than giving their lives to others in mission. Let us not allow ourselves to be robbed of missionary enthusiasm! (80)

He goes on to point out how dangerous this can be for those who work for the Church. As it becomes more a career than a ministry to God's people, the dangers increase:

> The problem is not always an excess of activity, but rather activity undertaken badly, without adequate motivation, without a spirituality which would permeate it and make it pleasurable. As a result, work becomes more tiring than necessary, even leading at times to illness. Far from a content and happy tiredness, this is a tense, burdensome, dissatisfying and, in the end, unbearable fatigue. (82)

While this is more of a problem for professionals in the Church, it can become a problem for anyone who is seeking to take a more intentional approach to sharing the Gospel with others. There's a sort of spiritual burnout that can spread from those who are working in the field full-time. An overexposure to the Church in the news can also lead to a jaded and cynical view. The news media isn't always the best filter for spiritual matters. But all of us, lay and clergy, can lose track of the need to take time for prayer and encountering Christ.

For Pope Francis, the best solution to this problem lies in a very human and direct encounter with Christ present in the people around us. It can seem counterintuitive, but the truth of it is proven again and again if we take the chance of stepping out of our ruts. A wise spiritual director will often respond to complaints of ennui and depression with a pointed question: "What are you doing to get outside of yourself?" Pope Francis has recognized this phenomenon on a Church-wide level.

> We need to avoid it by making the Church constantly go out from herself, keeping her mission focused on Jesus Christ, and her commitment to the poor. God save us from a worldly Church with superficial spiritual and pastoral trappings! This stifling worldliness can only be healed by breathing in the pure air of the Holy Spirit who frees us from self-centredness cloaked in an outward religiosity bereft of God. Let us not allow ourselves to be robbed of the Gospel! (97)

This avoidance of real human contact might be a particular issue of our increasingly technological age. The pope has been photographed taking a "selfie" with a group of young Catholics and has a Twitter account (@Pontifex), but he clearly recognizes the dangers of too much online interaction and not enough real life:

For just as some people want a purely spiritual Christ, without flesh and without the cross, they also want their interpersonal relationships provided by sophisticated equipment, by screens and systems which can be turned on and off on command. Meanwhile, the Gospel tells us constantly to run the risk of a face-to-face encounter with others, with their physical presence which challenges us, with their pain and their pleas, with their joy which infects us in our close and continuous interaction. (88)

Sharing the message of the Gospel always comes down to one thing: a personal encounter with Jesus Christ through his word, his presence in the Eucharist, and his presence in other people. And the pope, the Bishop of Rome, the pastor of the universal Church, never lets his advice stray too far into the theoretical realm. In the midst of his apostolic exhortation on evangelization, he makes it clear that the core of this task is something very concrete, but no less of a challenge:

We all have our likes and dislikes, and perhaps at this very moment we are angry with someone. At least let us say to the Lord: "Lord, I am angry with this person, with that person. I pray to you for him and for her". To pray for a person with whom I am irritated is a beautiful step forward in love, and an act of evangelization. Let us do it today! Let us not allow ourselves to be robbed of the ideal of fraternal love! (101)

Joy in Action

Take some time to explore some of the hot-button issues in the Church today. Try to set aside preconceived ideas, whether your own, someone else's, or those of the media, and approach these issues with an open mind. Bring the light of faith to bear on these issues. Ask yourself how Jesus might respond.

Few people would argue that the clergy sex abuse crisis has not had a significant impact on the way we view the institutional Church. In order to evangelize successfully, we need to confront this issue and deal with the spiritual and emotional impact is has had on so many people. Some have said it's the single greatest challenge facing Pope Francis and the Church. Take some time to think about how this issue has affected you. How might you move forward?

CHAPTER FIVE

"LET US BEGIN AGAIN"
Returning to the Word of God

I
t can be easy to feel discouraged by the challenges that come
from both the secular world and the all too human weaknesses
and failures of the institutional Church. When Jesus told his
disciples that they were in the world but not of the world, he knew
what he was talking about. We live in a sometimes uneasy tension
between heaven and earth. But this is where we find ourselves and
this is where we encounter God. Sometimes the best antidote to what
Wordsworth described as "the world is too much with us" is taking
time apart to reconnect with the word of God. A friend of mine
often responds to some litany of complaints and frustrations with the
simple question, "Are you able to take it to prayer?" It doesn't take me
long to recognize what's missing in my life at that moment.

One of the things that people have noticed about the seemingly
extraordinary words and deeds of our new pope is that they're very
much the things that Jesus himself said and did. In spite of the popu-
larity a few years ago of the WWJD movement, too often the words
and actions of people who profess to be religious and Christian are
a far cry from those of the man they profess to follow. Whether it's
an ostentatious lifestyle or being quick to judge and even condemn
others for their sins, church people are as likely as anyone else to fall

away from the ideal they strive to meet. The fact that Pope Francis has seemed so refreshingly different from what we've come to expect should tell us something about our need to get back to Gospel basics. We need to remind ourselves of what God's word tells us so that when we go into the world, we will recognize the divine challenge in our daily lives: "The Church must be a place of mercy freely given, where everyone can feel welcomed, loved, forgiven and encouraged to live the good life of the Gospel" (114).

A significant section of The Joy of the Gospel is addressed to priests and deacons who do formal preaching at Mass. One thing that this tells us is that even if we're only listening to the homily on Sundays, we have a right to a high-quality homily. Too many people are willing to settle for far less than they deserve. They no longer bother to pay attention because they won't hear anything that speaks to the real and deep needs in their lives. Pope Francis is not the first to address this issue. The U.S. bishops as well as previous popes have addressed this need for genuine proclamation and interpretation of God's word. Perhaps if ordinary Catholics listen in on some of this advice, they'll have a better understanding of the dissatisfaction they may feel with less-than-stellar homilies.

Somewhat tongue in cheek, Pope Francis raises the topic of preaching in this way:

> The homily is the touchstone for judging a pastor's closeness and ability to communicate to his people. We know that the faithful attach great importance to it, and that both they and their ordained ministers suffer because of homilies: the laity from having to listen to them and the clergy from having to preach them! It is sad that this is the case. The homily can actually be an intense and happy experience of the Spirit, a

consoling encounter with God's word, a constant source of renewal and growth. (135)

He goes on to point out that while biblical interpretation is a key element in successful preaching, it will fail to inspire unless it connects the word of God with the life of the people:

> The preacher also needs to keep his ear to the people and to discover what it is that the faithful need to hear. A preacher has to contemplate the word, but he also has to contemplate his people.... He needs to be able to link the message of a biblical text to a human situation, to an experience which cries out for the light of God's word. (154)

Even the pope can't guarantee that our parish priests will all be outstanding homilists. But that doesn't let us off the hook in encountering God in the sacred Scriptures. We need to let God's word evangelize our own hearts and minds on a continual basis. This isn't something that we learn once and then set aside. Like Jesus retreating to the mountains to pray and converse with his Father, we need to return again and again to the well of sacred Scripture. There, like Jacob, we wrestle with the Lord. We learn to speak in God's name with the humility of the prophets.

In chapter one, we looked to the Gospels as the primary place to encounter Jesus Christ and become familiar with his life and ministry. In this chapter, it's time to look at the lives and calling of the prophets and the apostles, because we too are called to speak God's word to the people around us. We too are sent forth to proclaim the Good News. It can be helpful to look to these biblical role models.

The Acts of the Apostles give us numerous examples of the way the first disciples of Jesus took the message he gave them and shared it with others. Reading about their adventures, we might be daunted by their great success, as thousands are converted and baptized on an almost daily basis. But we also discover that they had failures and challenges along the way. Pope Francis reminds us that each generation of Christians has faced obstacles to evangelization:

> We do well to keep in mind the early Christians and our many brothers and sisters throughout history who were filled with joy, unflagging courage and zeal in proclaiming the Gospel. Some people nowadays console themselves by saying that things are not as easy as they used to be, yet we know that the Roman empire was not conducive to the Gospel message, the struggle for justice, or the defence of human dignity. Every period of history is marked by the presence of human weakness, self-absorption, complacency and selfishness, to say nothing of the concupiscence which preys upon us all. These things are ever present under one guise or another; they are due to our human limits rather than particular situations. Let us not say, then, that things are harder today; they are simply different. (263)

If the Acts of the Apostles gives us something of a how-to guide to evangelization, the Hebrew prophets remind us that God's people have always needed a bit of prodding to stay on the path to God. They also give us some foundation for the inevitable ways in which we need to challenge the world around us, especially in the areas of caring for the poor and the oppressed. Passages from prophets such as Isaiah, Jeremiah, Amos, Hosea, and Micah are frequently paired with the Gospel readings at Sunday Mass to put Jesus's words into the context of his religious heritage. Whether he's challenging secular leaders, religious teachers, or his own disciples, his message is consistent with that of God's greatest prophets. If you're relatively unfamiliar with the Old Testament, you might want to begin with those passages from the Sunday lectionary. They have been chosen to speak to a contemporary audience without becoming bogged down in the sometimes confusing historical contexts of the ancient Hebrew societies.

Praying with the Bible

The pope's words reveal that he has an intimate and lifelong relationship with the Bible. He says;

> With this newness [Jesus] is always able to renew our lives and our communities, and even if the Christian message has known periods of darkness and ecclesial weakness, it will never grow old. Jesus can also break through the dull categories with which we would enclose him and he constantly amazes us by his divine creativity. Whenever we make the effort to return to the source and to recover the original freshness of the Gospel, new avenues arise, new paths of creativity open up, with different forms of expression, more eloquent signs and words with new meaning for today's world. Every form of authentic evangelization is always "new." (11)

The pope offers a tried-and-true method of praying with Scripture. If we do nothing more than make an effort to apply these questions to the Sunday readings on a regular and intentional basis, we will be well on the way to nourishing our own spiritual lives. We will hear God's call to joy and respond to it by sharing that joy with all those we meet.

> To interpret a biblical text, we need to be patient, to put aside all other concerns, and to give it our time, interest and undivided attention. We must leave aside any other pressing

concerns and create an environment of serene concentration. It is useless to attempt to read a biblical text if all we are looking for are quick, easy and immediate results.

In the presence of God, during a recollected reading of the text, it is good to ask, for example: "Lord, what does this text say to me?"

"What is it about my life that you want to change by this text?"

"What troubles me about this text? Why am I not interested in this?"

Or perhaps: "What do I find pleasant in this text? What is it about this word that moves me? What attracts me? Why does it attract me?"

When we make an effort to listen to the Lord, temptations usually arise. One of them is simply to feel troubled or burdened, and to turn away. Another common temptation is to think about what the text means for other people, and so avoid applying it to our own life.

It can also happen that we look for excuses to water down the clear meaning of the text. Or we can wonder if God is demanding too much of us, asking for a decision which we are not yet prepared to make. This leads many people to stop taking pleasure in the encounter with God's word; but this would mean forgetting that no one is more patient than God our Father, that no one is more understanding and willing to wait.

He always invites us to take a step forward, but does not demand a full response if we are not yet ready. He simply asks that we sincerely look at our life and present ourselves honestly before him, and that we be willing to continue to grow, asking from him what we ourselves cannot as yet achieve. (153)

Try this method with a few passages from the Bible. You might want to do this over several days or even several weeks. Keep track of some of your responses and whether these change over time. Notice how your reactions to the word of God vary depending on what else is happening in your life.

Joy in Action

Establish some daily routines for encountering God in Scripture. The one that holds pride of place in the Church's tradition is the Liturgy of the Hours. This practice of "praying with the Church" is known by other names—the Breviary, the Divine Office—and was once thought to be the privilege of vowed religious. If it is unfamiliar to you, it can be intimidating at first, but don't be discouraged. Find a good guide (Daria Sockey's book, *The Everyday Catholic's Guide to the Liturgy of the Hours,* is excellent) or an online source or app (Universalis.com or iBreviary) and start slowly.

Sometimes we're overwhelmed by words. The information age can bombard us with text. Another place to encounter Christ is in Eucharistic Adoration. As Catholics, we believe in the real presence of Christ in the Eucharist. Pope Francis, like so many people before him, has a firm commitment to spending time in prayer before the Eucharist. This might seem odd or awkward if we're not familiar with it or if we come from a non-Catholic background. But if you give it a fair trial, you might discover some amazing graces that flow from this time-honored practice.

CHAPTER SIX

"BLESSED ARE THE POOR"
The Special Place of the Poor and Vulnerable

O ne of the key ideas to come out of various Latin American
Church documents in the middle of the twentieth century
was the "preferential option for the poor." This wasn't a
new idea by any stretch of the imagination. It goes all the way back to
the Hebrew Scriptures and God taking a small remnant of nomads
and making them his chosen people. And every time they got too
rich and powerful, they forgot their need for God, who then sent the
prophets to call them back to being faithful. And Jesus in the Gospels
has a thing or two to say to poor and lowly, as well as to the rich and
exalted. So the Church in Latin America was reflecting on that heritage and applying it to the lives of the poor and oppressed people in
in our contemporary society. The witness of Scripture assures us that
God's concern is always for the poor, those who know their dependence of God for their very lives.

Pope Francis from the first days of his election has made it clear
that the special place of the poor is one of the keys to his papacy. His
very choice of the name Francis was inspired by Cardinal Hummes of
Brazil leaning over to him as the votes were being tallied and saying,
"Don't forget about the poor." Much of his ministry as an archbishop
and cardinal in Buenos Aires was spent reaching out to the poor in

the slum parishes. He walked among them and felt privileged to be accepted into their neighborhoods and homes.

It's natural, then, that this idea has a strong representation in The Joy of the Gospel:

> This is why I want a Church which is poor and for the poor. They have much to teach us. Not only do they share in the *sensus fidei*, but in their difficulties they know the suffering Christ. We need to let ourselves be evangelized by them. The new evangelization is an invitation to acknowledge the saving power at work in their lives and to put them at the centre of the Church's pilgrim way. We are called to find Christ in them, to lend our voice to their causes, but also to be their friends, to listen to them, to speak for them and to embrace the mysterious wisdom which God wishes to share with us through them.

This approach begins with an attitude of reverence for the poor just as they are. With little social status to recommend them, we can quickly recognize that their worth stems almost entirely from their very beings. They are created by and beloved of God through no effort or achievement of their own. This might be one of the most challenging concepts for American Catholics to recognize. We've spent decades working our way out of the Catholic ghetto to some of the highest business and political offices in the country. A reminder of how much God loves the poor is not always the most welcome sentiment from our Church leaders.

Pope Francis points again and again to the special gifts that the poor have to offer to the rest of the Church. While charity and justice urge us toward greater equality, it's not necessarily a question of making the poor like us, with our complacency and our comfortable middle class lives. The poor know a deep dependency on God that flows from their dependency on other people. They lack our false idol of self-sufficiency.

He clearly has a deep understanding of the poor because he has lived with them, walked with them, eaten with them, celebrated liturgy with them on a daily basis. He continues to find ways to do this even in Rome as the head of the universal Church. It is a witness that can't be ignored, and it emerges from the words and actions of Jesus himself.

A Simple Faith

One of the ways that the poor can teach us something about how to encounter God, says Pope Francis, is through their simple forms of piety. What many would dismiss as cultural superstition or sentimental kitsch, the pope recognizes as having significance on a much different level. It's a good corrective for those of us who spend too much time in our intellects.

> Genuine forms of popular religiosity are incarnate, since they are born of the incarnation of Christian faith in popular culture. For this reason they entail a personal relationship, not with vague spiritual energies or powers, but with God, with Christ, with Mary, with the saints. These devotions are fleshy, they have a face. They are capable of fostering relationships and not just enabling escapism. In other parts of our society, we see the growing attraction to various forms of a "spirituality of well-being" divorced from any community life, or to a "theology of prosperity" detached from responsibility for our brothers and sisters, or to depersonalized

experiences which are nothing more than a form of self-centredness. (90)

Perhaps the best way to grasp this sacramental, incarnational spirituality is to look at the way we pray when we are in psychological and emotional turmoil. When we or a loved one is sick, in danger, or dying, the theological constructs and complex prayers behind which we sometimes hide from God lose all their appeal. We grasp for a much more basic, intuitive way to connect with the divine strength we so desperately need:

> To understand this reality we need to approach it with the gaze of the Good Shepherd, who seeks not to judge but to love.... I think of the steadfast faith of those mothers tending their sick children who, though perhaps barely familiar with the articles of the creed, cling to a rosary; or of all the hope poured into a candle lighted in a humble home with a prayer for help from Mary, or in the gaze of tender love directed to Christ crucified. (125)

This tendency to pray with "things" is almost exclusive to Catholicism and often criticized by more fundamentalist Christians. It is part of our belief in the holiness or sacramentality of creation. Water, oil, bread, human touch—these things form the basis of our seven sacraments and countless devotional prayers and actions. It's not surprising that they are most easily grasped and accepted by people who feel no self-conscious need to explain and justify them.

The Cry of Justice

If the spiritual witness of the poor plays a role in the new evangelization, the cry of justice for the oppressed is the other side of that coin, and it has a role from the days of the Hebrew prophets. If God has a special love for the poor, that love causes him to demand that his people share in his concern by providing for the poorest and most vulnerable in society. In the Old Testament, these were represented by widows and orphans, two groups that were utterly helpless in a patriarchal society with no men to provide for them. In our day, many groups fall into this category: homeless people, immigrants, those with disabilities, those who struggle with addictions. All the people that society has decided don't contribute their fair share to the bottom line can fall through the cracks of our not-always-kind social welfare programs.

> It is essential to draw near to new forms of poverty and vulnerability, in which we are called to recognize the suffering Christ, even if this appears to bring us no tangible and immediate benefits. I think of the homeless, the addicted, refugees, indigenous peoples, the elderly who are increasingly isolated and abandoned, and many others. Migrants present a particular challenge for me, since I am the pastor of a Church without frontiers, a Church which considers herself mother to all. For this reason, I exhort all countries to a generous openness which, rather than fearing the loss of local identity, will prove capable of creating new forms of cultural synthesis. How beautiful are those cities which overcome paralysing mistrust, integrate those who are different and make this very integration a new factor of development! How attractive are those cities which, even in their architectural design, are full of spaces which connect, relate and favour the recognition of others! (210)

The Church has long recognized and advocated for the poor. Our care for them through both charitable efforts and lobbying for just solutions is one of the shining lights of Catholicism. The pope's words in The Joy of the Gospel are merely the latest in a long line of Catholic social teaching. But the clarity of his message, largely free of theological jargon, and the example of his actions may give these words new life and greater impact in our jaded society.

> We can understand Jesus' command to his disciples: "You yourselves give them something to eat!" (Mk 6:37): it means working to eliminate the structural causes of poverty and to promote the integral development of the poor, as well as small daily acts of solidarity in meeting the real needs which we encounter. The word "solidarity" is a little worn and at times poorly understood, but it refers to something more than a few sporadic acts of generosity. It presumes the creation of a new mindset which thinks in terms of community and the priority of the life of all over the appropriation of goods by a few. (188)

The pope goes on to explain what he means by solidarity with the poor. He is quite clear that the common good takes priority over private property:

> Solidarity is a spontaneous reaction by those who recognize that the social function of property and the universal destination of goods are realities which come before private property. The private ownership of goods is justified by the need to protect and increase them, so that they can better serve the common good; for this reason, solidarity must be lived as the decision to restore to the poor what belongs to them. (189)

The reference to restoring to the poor what belongs to them reminds me of the fourth-century St. Basil the Great, who said,

> The bread which you do not use is the bread of the hungry; the garment hanging in your wardrobe is the garment of him who is naked; the shoes that you do not wear are the shoes of the one who is barefoot; the money that you keep locked away is the money of the poor; the acts of charity that you do not perform are so many injustices that you commit.

These are strong words, and no less true because we find them disturbing. Like the Gospels, the words of the great prophets and holy men and women in our tradition often make us uncomfortable.

Jesus told the rich man to sell what he had and give to the poor, a command St. Francis of Assisi took quite seriously. We sometimes gloss over these stories or try to explain that Jesus didn't really mean what he seems to be saying. We spiritualize the Gospel references to money. This is more difficult to do when Pope Francis's makes statement in contemporary economic terms:

> We can no longer trust in the unseen forces and the invisible hand of the market. Growth in justice requires more than economic growth, while presupposing such growth: it requires decisions, programmes, mechanisms and processes specifically geared to a better distribution of income, the creation of sources of employment and an integral promotion of the poor which goes beyond a simple welfare mentality. (204)

This statement was quickly denounced by the pope's critics, some of whom pointed out that of course coming from Argentina he doesn't understand the U.S. capitalist economy. But it's clear from other contexts that the pope says what he means and means what he says.

The pope points out that the best kind of justice will enable the poor to have meaningful work:

> This means education, access to health care, and above all employment, for it is through free, creative, participatory and mutually supportive labour that human beings express and enhance the dignity of their lives. A just wage enables them to have adequate access to all the other goods which are destined for our common use. (192)

My college ethics professor defined economic justice as the ability not only to survive but to thrive a little. St. Francis encouraged his friars to work with their hands and always preferred working to simply begging for their daily bread. The dignity of work is something that we can have a tendency to devalue in our quest for leisure and labor-saving devices. If the goal of wealthy people is to be able to afford to hire someone to do all of their menial tasks, what message does this send to the poor other than that work is something to be avoided? Pope Francis emphasizes that all kinds of work have one goal: the common good of all people. He writes:

> The dignity of each human person and the pursuit of the common good are concerns which ought to shape all economic policies.... Business is a vocation, and a noble vocation, provided that those engaged in it see themselves challenged by a greater meaning in life; this will enable them truly to serve the common good by striving to increase the goods of this world and to make them more accessible to all. (203)

The Dignity of All People

Pope Francis calls attention to the crime of human trafficking, something that takes place throughout the world but has been a particular scourge in the cities of his South American homeland:

> I have always been distressed at the lot of those who are victims of various kinds of human trafficking. How I wish that all of us would hear God's cry: "Where is your brother?" (Gen 4:9). Where is your brother or sister who is enslaved? Where is the brother and sister whom you are killing each day in clandestine warehouses, in rings of prostitution, in children used for begging, in exploiting undocumented labour? Let us not look the other way. There is greater complicity than we think. The issue involves everyone! This infamous network of crime is now well established in our cities, and many people have blood on their hands as a result of their comfortable and silent complicity. Doubly poor are those women who endure situations of exclusion, mistreatment and violence, since they are frequently less able to defend their rights. Even so, we constantly witness among them impressive examples of daily heroism in defending and protecting their vulnerable families. (211–212)

Finally, the pope makes it clear that defense of the unborn is and will always be of special concern to the Church:

> Among the vulnerable for whom the Church wishes to care with particular love and concern are unborn children, the most defenceless and innocent among us. Nowadays efforts are made to deny them their human dignity and to do with them whatever one pleases, taking their lives and passing

laws preventing anyone from standing in the way of this. Frequently, as a way of ridiculing the Church's effort to defend their lives, attempts are made to present her position as ideological, obscurantist and conservative. Yet this defence of unborn life is closely linked to the defence of each and every other human right. It involves the conviction that a human being is always sacred and inviolable, in any situation and at every stage of development. Human beings are ends in themselves and never a means of resolving other problems. (213)

Where this pope makes his own mark on the Church's teaching in this fundamental human rights question is in his ability to bring a hotly debated topic into a very human and personal realm. He makes it clear that the Church's position on abortion cannot and should not change. But the wisdom of the pastor comes through in his reflection on the further work that is required:

> On the other hand, it is also true that we have done little to adequately accompany women in very difficult situations, where abortion appears as a quick solution to their profound anguish, especially when the life developing within them is the result of rape or a situation of extreme poverty. Who can remain unmoved before such painful situations? (214)

This element of compassion for the people involved and the complexity of a situation where no one wins sometimes seems to be missing when rhetoric and screaming across the barricades are the only means of communication.

Joy in Action

Reflect on the beatitudes from the Sermon on the Mount (Matthew 5—7) or the Sermon on the Plain (Luke 6). For each one, think of a concrete contemporary comparison. Whom do you know that best exemplifies the idea of "poor in spirit"? Where are those who hunger and thirst for righteousness in your community? Notice that Jesus says that these people are blessed here and now. How does this overturn our normal expectations about happiness and blessedness? How did St. Francis understand this idea?

Matthew 25 is a key passage to consider when we look at the special place of the poor and vulnerable. What is it asking us to do? What concrete steps can you take to perform these corporal works of mercy?

"STEWARDS OF CREATION"
Peace and the Common Good

Christianity began with a small group of Galilean fishermen who had encountered the presence of God in a carpenter from the town of Nazareth. The death and resurrection of the Son of God was the spark that set a fire from Jerusalem to Rome and throughout the whole world. This movement takes place in each one of us. We encounter Jesus in the Gospels, in the Church, in the people who love us and listen to us and challenge us to go out and share what we have heard. The message of the Gospel has never been meant as a personal reassurance of salvation. From the time Jesus told his disciples, "What you have received as gift, give as gift," our mission has been clear.

Reading the Scriptures also makes it clear that the Gospel is not merely about our personal relationship with God. Nor should our loving response to God be seen simply as an accumulation of small personal gestures to individuals in need, a kind of "charity à la carte", or a series of acts aimed solely at easing our conscience. The Gospel is about the kingdom of God (cf. Lk 4:43); it is about loving God who reigns in our world. To the extent that he reigns within us, the life of society will be a setting for universal fraternity, justice, peace and dignity. Both Christian preaching and life, then, are meant to have an impact on society. (180)

One of my favorite quotes from St. Catherine of Siena is, "If you are who you are meant to be, you will set the world on fire." The first apostles experienced this at Pentecost. We experience it every time we let people know that what inspires us is the divine gift of grace, a gift that is freely given to each and every one of them as well. Because we have been called by God and loved by God, it is up to us to share that love with the whole world—no exceptions.

Many Vatican observers have suggested that Pope Francis's next major encyclical could be on the theme of the environment. This has certainly been one of the themes running through his first year as pope. The Vatican in the last few decades has been increasingly setting an example of conservation, ecology, and care for creation. There is no more overarching example of "the common good" than the air we breathe, the water we drink, and the earth that sustains us:

An authentic faith—which is never comfortable or completely personal—always involves a deep desire to change the world, to transmit values, to leave this earth somehow better that we found it. We love this magnificent planet on which God has put us, and we love the human family which dwells here, with all its tragedies and struggles, its hopes and aspirations, its strengths and weaknesses. The earth is our common home and all of us are brothers and sisters. (183)

We human beings are not only the beneficiaries but also the stewards of other creatures. Thanks to our bodies, God has joined us so closely to the world around us that we can feel the desertification of the soil almost as a physical ailment, and the extinction of a species as a painful disfigurement. Let us not leave in our wake a swath of destruction and death which will affect our own lives and those of future generations. (215)

Pope Francis makes it clear in his exhortation that it is up to us to care for the world: "Small yet strong in the love of God, like Saint Francis of Assisi, all of us, as Christians, are called to watch over and protect the fragile world in which we live, and all its peoples" (216). Once again the message of peace must spread from Rome throughout the known world.

When Pope Francis issued his call for people to set aside September 7, 2013, to fast and pray for peace in Syria, I found myself tempted to dismiss it as a predictable and idealistic response to a disturbingly complex situation. I had to knock down a few cynical arguments in my head ("Right, because God won't do anything about the situation unless enough people pray and fast!"). Then Saturday rolled around, I had a day at home, and I simply gave myself over to the pope's intention.

I tuned in to the live broadcast from Vatican TV on YouTube. I wanted to participate in this vigil for peace without commentary or interpretation. I had spent the better part of three days in St. Peter's Square two years ago, and I had almost a physical memory of the dimensions of the area. I truly felt as though I was gathered with those praying in Rome and around the world. The Internet has made the idea of a universal Church much more accessible and real.

The first thing that struck me was the recitation of the joyful mysteries of the rosary. It seemed incongruous, and yet it was a reminder that Jesus was born into a world similarly troubled by war, oppression, and the misuse of power. The phrase that hit me over the head was from the annunciation story in Luke's Gospel: "Nothing is impossible with God."

The line that stayed with me from Pope Francis's homily was this: "In the silence of the Cross, the uproar of weapons ceases and the language of reconciliation, forgiveness, dialogue, and peace is spoken." I realized that fasting and praying aren't about changing God's mind or even about changing the circumstances or the outcome. But even more, I realized that as a Christian and a Franciscan, I can't make a choice for violence, ever. It was a humbling and yet strangely reassuring thought.

After the Adoration of the Eucharist, the reading from John's Gospel recounted the story of Jesus appearing to the disciples in the Upper Room after the resurrection. The witness of the Church from the beginning is that God can always bring life out of death and destruction.

The message communicated so powerfully on that day, which has yet to bear practical fruit in the troubled world of the Middle East, remains as an ideal and a goal. The significance of it runs through The Joy of the Gospel:

> Peace in society cannot be understood as pacification or the mere absence of violence resulting from the domination of one part of society over others. Nor does true peace act as a pretext for justifying a social structure which silences or appeases the poor, so that the more affluent can placidly support their lifestyle while others have to make do as they can. Demands involving the distribution of wealth, concern for the poor and human rights cannot be suppressed under the guise of creating a consensus on paper or a transient

peace for a contented minority. The dignity of the human person and the common good rank higher than the comfort of those who refuse to renounce their privileges. When these values are threatened, a prophetic voice must be raised. (218)

Like any gifted preacher, Pope Francis is adept at moving between world issues and personal issues. We cannot profess to be committed to peace in the world if we cannot consistently maintain peace in our hearts and in our personal relationships. Much of what he says about the need to resolve conflicts can apply just as well to our everyday lives as to the countries featured on the evening news: "Conflict cannot be ignored or concealed. It has to be faced. But if we remain trapped in conflict, we lose our perspective, our horizons shrink and reality itself begins to fall apart. In the midst of conflict, we lose our sense of the profound unity of reality" (226).

Too many times I've let myself be distracted by conflicts at home, at work, among my family and friends. I find the pope's words to be both comforting and challenging. I probably fall into his second example below. Rarely am I untouched by conflict, but neither do I consistently move through it.

> When conflict arises, some people simply look at it and go their way as if nothing happened; they wash their hands of it and get on with their lives. Others embrace it in such a way that they become its prisoners; they lose their bearings, project onto institutions their own confusion and dissatisfaction and thus make unity impossible. But there is also a third way, and it is the best way to deal with conflict. It is the willingness to face conflict head on, to resolve it and to make it a link in the chain of a new process. "Blessed are the peacemakers!" (Mt 5:9). (227)

Sometimes we need to begin with small steps, finding ways to reduce conflict and violence in our own lives. Again, St. Francis becomes a role model not only for the pope but for each of us. He made peace with himself, abandoning his dreams of a military career. He confronted warring factions in Assisi and Perugia. In time he was able to reach out to the Sultan of Baghdad in an attempt to reconcile the escalating catastrophe of the Crusades.

We've all heard the phrase, "Think globally but act locally." Pope Francis fleshes out this slogan in The Joy of the Gospel:

> We constantly have to broaden our horizons and see the greater good which will benefit us all. But this has to be done without evasion or uprooting. We need to sink our roots deeper into the fertile soil and history of our native place, which is a gift of God. We can work on a small scale, in our own neighbourhood, but with a larger perspective. Nor do people who wholeheartedly enter into the life of a community need to lose their individualism or hide their identity; instead, they receive new impulses to personal growth. The global need not stifle, nor the particular prove barren. (235)

Again and again he brings us back to the central teaching of Jesus, the mission to go out to the world and share what we have discovered: "The Gospel has an intrinsic principle of totality: it will always remain good news until it has been proclaimed to all people, until it has healed and strengthened every aspect of humanity, until it has brought all men and women together at table in God's kingdom" (237).

Joy in Action

World peace can sometimes seem like a completely unattainable goal. We look at issues such as war and the environment, and we despair.

But there are always steps that we can take, however insignificant they might seem.

Check the Vatican website each month for the pope's special prayer intentions. We get so caught up in "saying prayers" that sometimes we lose sight of how effective real prayer can be. It's not something we do to change God's mind. It's something we do to change ourselves, to bring ourselves more and more in line with God's will.

The concept of the "common good" is something that we're in danger of losing as our societies become more technologically sophisticated. We begin to think that we don't need other human beings as long as we have our computers and, increasingly, robots and artificial intelligence. Pope Francis reminds us not to lose the human element in all of these advances. Make sure you turn off your gadgets from time to time and enjoy the simple pleasures of family, friends, pets, and hobbies.

The Church for the past few decades has been an increasingly committed voice in the debate over global climate change and the need to care for the environment. Consider your own stance on these issues and how you will respond to the challenge.

CHAPTER EIGHT

"THE KINGDOM IS HERE"
A Renewed Impulse to Share Our Faith

We think of evangelization as something a bit scary, not quite Catholic, door-to-door missionaries and street corner preachers. But Pope Francis is trying to show us that it can be the most natural thing in the world. Don't start by walking up to strangers. What about those "spiritual but not religious" acquaintances in your circle? What might you say to them? A priest friend of mine (admittedly a gifted preacher) once said that he appreciates the opportunity to celebrate the funeral mass for a young person because he knows that so many of the people in the congregation are young people searching for the truth.

Pope Francis himself is creating a wonderful opportunity for evangelization to take place, simply because nearly every day, people are talking about him. He's in the news or someone has a quote on their Facebook feed. The opportunity for conversation is there. People are open to him in a way that they haven't been in a very long time. Partly this is because he listens without judging, admits that other people can have answers he hasn't thought of.

In many ways, Pope Francis is the ideal man for our times. He's open and gregarious, he's not afraid to say what he thinks, he's pastoral, and he's open to the media (often before his press office is even aware of it). And there's a consistency in his thinking and in what he says and does. Many of his answers from his interview with *America* are included in his apostolic exhortation. He's willing to talk to journalists instead of seeing them as the enemy, although he acknowledges that the media often gets things wrong. You don't always agree with him, but he's earned the right to be listened to and taken seriously. He's a pastor of the universal Church in the best sense of the word.

I grew up in a fairly typical Catholic family in the upper Midwest. I went to Catholic schools from first grade through college. All my friends were Catholic. Among my nieces and nephews, we have a wide range of religious affiliations, including some "nones." And yet often they challenge those of us who regard ourselves as "churchy" with a much deeper commitment to charity and kindness. I still move in predominantly Catholic circles, but I have a much wider range of friends and acquaintances. Knowing how to present my faith to these people can be a challenge at times. Most of the time, I simply strive to be honest about who I am and what I believe. I would rather preach by example of what is right than by telling others that they're wrong. And I believe that sometimes just the fact that I am openly and unabashedly Catholic and yet accept my friends for who they are, Catholic or not, religious or not, is a witness to a God who welcomes everyone.

> Christians have the duty to proclaim the Gospel without excluding anyone. Instead of seeming to impose new obligations, they should appear as people who wish to share their joy, who point to a horizon of beauty and who invite others to a delicious banquet. It is not by proselytizing that the Church grows, but "by attraction". (13)

The Joy of the Gospel is an apostolic exhortation, but this is far more than merely its literary form or its classification among the hierarchy of Church documents. Pope Francis is sincerely exhorting us to be apostles, sent forth to proclaim the Good News of God's love, mercy, and forgiveness. We are all called to preach this message through our actions even more than our words. And each of us has a gift for doing this in our own unique ways, according to our personalities, our circumstances, and the particular people God brings into our lives.

Today, as the Church seeks to experience a profound missionary renewal, there is a kind of preaching which falls to each of us as a daily responsibility. It has to do with bringing the Gospel to the people we meet, whether they be our neighbours or complete strangers. This is the informal preaching which takes place in the middle of a conversation, something along the lines of what a missionary does when visiting a home. Being a disciple means being constantly ready to bring the love of Jesus to others, and this can happen unexpectedly and in any place: on the street, in a city square, during work, on a journey. (127)

As we close this reflection this first significant document of Francis's papacy, we might simply take time to read and reflect on his closing words in the document. They are neither lofty nor academic. They need little explanation or interpretation.

Action and Contemplation

Spirit-filled evangelizers are evangelizers who pray and work. Mystical notions without a solid social and missionary outreach are of no help to evangelization, nor are dissertations or social or pastoral practices which lack a spirituality which can change hearts.... Without prolonged moments of adoration, of prayerful encounter with the word, of sincere

conversation with the Lord, our work easily becomes meaningless; we lose energy as a result of weariness and difficulties, and our fervour dies out. The Church urgently needs the
deep breath of prayer, and to my great joy groups devoted to
prayer and intercession, the prayerful reading of God's word
and the perpetual adoration of the Eucharist are growing at
every level of ecclesial life. (262)

Falling in Love

The primary reason for evangelizing is the love of Jesus
which we have received, the experience of salvation which
urges us to ever greater love of him. What kind of love would
not feel the need to speak of the beloved, to point him out,
to make him known? If we do not feel an intense desire to
share this love, we need to pray insistently that he will once
more touch our hearts. We need to implore his grace daily,
asking him to open our cold hearts and shake up our luke-
warm and superficial existence. Standing before him with
open hearts, letting him look at us, we see that gaze of love
which Nathaniel glimpsed on the day when Jesus said to
him: "I saw you under the fig tree" (Jn 1:48). How good it is
to stand before a crucifix, or on our knees before the Blessed
Sacrament, and simply to be in his presence! How much
good it does us when he once more touches our lives and
impels us to share his new life! What then happens is that
"we speak of what we have seen and heard" (1 Jn 1:3). The
best incentive for sharing the Gospel comes from contem-
plating it with love, lingering over its pages and reading it
with the heart. If we approach it in this way, its beauty will
amaze and constantly excite us. But if this is to come about,

we need to recover a contemplative spirit which can help us to realize ever anew that we have been entrusted with a treasure which makes us more human and helps us to lead a new life. There is nothing more precious which we can give to others. (264)

When the Going Gets Tough

Jesus' whole life, his way of dealing with the poor, his actions, his integrity, his simple daily acts of generosity, and finally his complete self-giving, is precious and reveals the mystery of his divine life…. Sometimes we lose our enthusiasm for mission because we forget that the Gospel responds to our deepest needs, since we were created for what the Gospel offers us: friendship with Jesus and love of our brothers and sisters. If we succeed in expressing adequately and with beauty the essential content of the Gospel, surely this message will speak to the deepest yearnings of people's hearts…. Enthusiasm for evangelization is based on this conviction. We have a treasure of life and love which cannot deceive, and a message which cannot mislead or disappoint. It penetrates to the depths of our hearts, sustaining and ennobling us. It is a truth which is never out of date because it reaches that part of us which nothing else can reach. Our infinite sadness can only be cured by an infinite love. (265)

We See in Others the Face of God

When we live out a spirituality of drawing nearer to others and seeking their welfare, our hearts are opened wide to the Lord's greatest and most beautiful gifts. Whenever we encounter another person in love, we learn something new about God. Whenever our eyes are opened to acknowledge the other, we grow in the light of faith and knowledge of God. If we want to advance in the spiritual life, then, we must constantly be missionaries. The work of evangelization enriches the mind and the heart; it opens up spiritual horizons; it makes us more and more sensitive to the workings of the Holy Spirit, and it takes us beyond our limited spiritual constructs. A committed missionary knows the joy of being a spring which spills over and refreshes others. Only the person who feels happiness in seeking the good of others, in desiring their happiness, can be a missionary. This openness of the heart is a source of joy, since "it is more blessed to give than to receive" (Acts 20:35). We do not live better when we flee, hide, refuse to share, stop giving and lock ourselves up in own comforts. Such a life is nothing less than slow suicide. (272)

If we are to share our lives with others and generously give of ourselves, we also have to realize that every person is worthy of our giving. Not for their physical appearance, their abilities, their language, their way of thinking, or for any satisfaction that we might receive, but rather because they are God's handiwork, his creation. God created that person in his image, and he or she reflects something of God's glory. Every human being is the object of God's infinite tenderness, and he himself is present in their lives. Jesus offered his precious blood on the cross for that person. Appearances notwithstanding, every person is immensely holy and deserves our love. Consequently, if I can help at least one person to have a better life, that already justifies the offering of my life. It is a wonderful thing to be God's faithful people. We achieve fulfilment when we break down walls and our heart is filled with faces and names! (274)

The Power of the Resurrection

Christ's resurrection is not an event of the past; it contains a vital power which has permeated this world. Where all seems to be dead, signs of the resurrection suddenly spring up. It is an irresistible force. Often it seems that God does not exist: all around us we see persistent injustice, evil, indifference and cruelty. But it is also true that in the midst of darkness something new always springs to life and sooner or later produces fruit. On razed land life breaks through, stubbornly yet invincibly. However dark things are, goodness always re-emerges and spreads. Each day in our world beauty is born anew, it rises transformed through the storms of history. Values always tend to reappear under new guises, and human beings have arisen time after time from situations that seemed doomed. Such is the power of the resurrection, and all who evangelize are instruments of that power. (276)

Faith also means believing in God, believing that he truly loves us, that he is alive, that he is mysteriously capable of intervening, that he does not abandon us and that he brings good out of evil by his power and his infinite creativity.... The kingdom is here, it returns, it struggles to flourish anew. Christ's resurrection everywhere calls forth seeds of that new world; even if they are cut back, they grow again, for the resurrection is already secretly woven into the fabric of this history, for Jesus did not rise in vain. May we never remain on the sidelines of this march of living hope! (278)

The Work is in God's Hands

Because we do not always see these seeds growing, we need an interior certainty, a conviction that God is able to act in every situation, even amid apparent setbacks: "We have this treasure in earthen vessels" (2 Cor 4:7). This certainty is often called "a sense of mystery". It involves knowing with certitude that all those who entrust themselves to God in love will bear good fruit (cf. Jn 15:5). This fruitfulness is often invisible, elusive and unquantifiable. We can know quite well that our lives will be fruitful, without claiming to know how, or where, or when. We may be sure that none of our acts of love will be lost, nor any of our acts of sincere concern for others. No single act of love for God will be lost, no generous effort is meaningless, no painful endurance is wasted. All of these encircle our world like a vital force. Sometimes it seems that our work is fruitless, but mission is not like a business transaction or investment, or even a humanitarian activity. It is not a show where we count how many people come as a result of our publicity; it is something much deeper, which escapes all measurement. It may be that the Lord uses our sacrifices to shower blessings in another part of the world which we will never visit. The Holy Spirit works as he wills, when he wills and where he wills; we entrust ourselves without pretending to see striking results. We know only that our commitment is necessary. Let us learn to rest in the tenderness of the arms of the Father amid our creative and generous commitment. Let us keep marching forward; let us give him everything, allowing him to make our efforts bear fruit in his good time. (279)

Joy in Action

Find a few quotes from Pope Francis and a few quotes from the Scriptures that speak deeply to your own experience of the joy of the Gospel. Look for opportunities to share them with the people you meet. Post them in a place where you will see them every morning.

ABOUT THE AUTHOR

Diane M. Houdek is the author of *Lent with St. Francis* and *Advent with St. Francis*. She has written for *Catholic Update, Bringing Home the Word* and *Homily Helps*.